Mark Twain at Home

STUDIES IN AMERICAN LITERARY REALISM AND NATURALISM

MARK TWAIN *at Home*

How Family Shaped Twain's Fiction

Michael J. Kiskis

Foreword by Laura Skandera Trombley

Afterword by Gary Scharnhorst

The University of Alabama Press ~ Tuscaloosa

The University of Alabama Press
Tuscaloosa, Alabama 35487-0380
uapress.ua.edu

Typeface: Garamond Premiere Pro

Manufactured in the United States of America
Cover image: Mark Twain with his family (*left to right*): Clara, Mark Twain, Jean, Livy (mother), and Susy; courtesy of the Mark Twain Project, Bancroft Library, University of California at Berkeley
Cover and interior design: Michele Myatt Quinn

∞

The paper on which this book is printed meets the minimum requirements of American National Standard for Information Sciences—Permanence of Paper for Printed Library Materials, ANSI Z39.48-1984.

Library of Congress Cataloging-in-Publication Data

Names: Kiskis, Michael J., author.

Title: Mark Twain at home : how family shaped Twain's fiction / Michael J. Kiskis; foreword by Laura Skandera Trombley ; afterword by Gary Scharnhorst.

Description: Tuscaloosa: University of Alabama Press, 2016. | Series: Studies in American literary realism and naturalism | Includes bibliographical references and index.

Identifiers: LCCN 2015041931| ISBN 9780817319151 (cloth : alk. paper) | ISBN 9780817389901 (e book)

Subjects: LCSH: Twain, Mark, 1835–1910—Criticism and interpretation. | Twain, Mark, 1835–1910—Homes and haunts. | Twain, Mark, 1835–1910—Family. | Home in literature. | Families in literature.

Classification: LCC PS1342.H55 K57 2016 | DDC 813/.409—dc23

LC record available at http://lccn.loc.gov/2015041931

For Ann

Contents

Foreword

Michael Kiskis, the "I," and Domesticity

Never refuse to do a kindness unless the act would work great injury to yourself, and never refuse to take a drink—under any circumstances.
—*Mark Twain's Notebook*

AND SO HERE I find myself, shortly before Mother's Day, writing about my dear friend Michael Kiskis, who died almost a year ago. Born on a holiday, the Fourth of July, he managed to exit on one as well: a nice pair of bookends that Twain would certainly appreciate. Over the course of the last twelve months I have quite deliberately tried to not think about his passing, although his death was finally ramrodded home to me this fall after something particularly absurd happened at my college. As I had done for decades, I automatically called Michael to share with him this latest bon mot from the precious world of academia and his number rang and rang until finally it hit me. Michael was dead, and no amount of denial on my part could change that hard fact. I pulled over to the side of the road and wept; in too many ways nothing will ever be quite as much fun anymore.

Without skating too far on analogically thin ice, Michael was in some ways similar to his favorite subject. Like Twain he had a tumultuous family life as a young boy. When Michael was fourteen, his father left, passing away shortly thereafter, and Michael was raised by his mother, who passed away in 1977. He was always quick to credit her for his love of education, as well as his awareness of the importance of hard work. Michael recalled that she had a "simple statement of principle: You learn and you use that learning to make your way. And you pay back, and make sure that others make their way." He believed academics had it soft, and this child of generations of millworkers would snicker when colleagues would complain of multiple committee assignments and demanding teaching loads. At times like these, he likely thought about his uncle, a factory millworker who accidentally had his right arm threaded into one of the weaving machines and always wore long-sleeve shirts around his family and relatives. In Michael's Catholic family, becoming a priest was considered the highest calling and teaching was favorably viewed as second best. Choosing a career as an academic, a writer and a thinker, was a much harder sell, and Michael recalled his mother warning him that he had best "find something else to do, a real job with real work."

Twain too had doubts about his choice of career, writing to his brother and sister-in-law, Orion and Mollie Clemens, in 1865: "I have had a 'call' to literature, of a low order—i.e., humorous. It is nothing to be proud of, but it is my strongest suit, & were I to listen to the maxim of stern duty which says to do right you must multiply the one of the two of the three talents which the almighty entrusts for your keeping, I would have long ago ceased to meddle with things for which I was by nature unfitted & turned my attention to seriously scribbling to excite the laughter of God's creatures. Poor pitiful business!"[1] Michael spent some serious time reflecting on how his working-class family background influenced his academic work, specifically his work on Twain. "Was it a choice?" Michael wondered. "Or was it, rather, a compulsion propelled by my identification with Clemens based on a constructed class identity (his and mine) and by a shared fear (his and mine) that we act as impostors within our professions." Michael liked to tell people that he was an academic because he was lazy, and then he would sit back and watch to see if they would take the bait.

Just as Twain created a persona, Michael in some ways did too. For years in public he played the affable ne'er-do-well, the everyman who was inclined to mock himself—a gift and occasionally an act of defiance, directed in particular toward those who take themselves too seriously. He became a touch point for the Twain scholarly community; you knew it was going to be a good conference/symposium/workshop/class/planning session/meeting if Michael was attending. Michael knew everyone and always had time for good conversation. Men liked him, women trusted him, and everyone teased him. As the years rolled by, he became the unofficial ambassador for Elmira's quadrennial Twain conference. For those of us who returned time after time to that blasted, rust-belt town whose heat index was as high as the humidity and whose demise was still being blamed on the flood of 1972, it was not long after check in at the decidedly pedestrian Holiday Inn that we were tempted to repack the rental and hit the road. There really was not enough liquor in the city limits for staying to make sense. For me—and I think for many of us—we stayed because of Michael. He often was among the organizers, and he was always ready to talk Twain, raise a glass, and have a good time.

He developed a reputation as a drinker, much like Twain: "Sometimes too much drink is barely enough." During the 1990s, Cabo San Lucas and Cancun were popular spots for American literature symposia. Those destinations were chosen because, as Alfred Bendixen rationalized it, Mexico was much less expensive than Cleveland and the drinks much stronger. It always struck Michael as odd that the most famous humorist in American literature drew the scrutiny of so many grim, mirthless academics. Cocktails were the antidotes to the seriousness of these conferences, and the bar became the place where a great and friendly community existed, one that resisted the skewering of the subject on theoretical pins, like a chloroformed butterfly of magnificent hue, and instead welcomed people of quick wit. Indeed, Michael and I were co-organizers of the now infamous conference, held in Cancun in 1996, "Male and Female Literary Relations in Nineteenth and Twentieth Century America," where panels were planned around cocktail hour and participants selected for their affability and the excellence of their scholarship and conversation. I recall on a different occasion in Cabo one hot and endless American Literature session where at exactly 5:00 p.m. the doors to the conference room burst open, thankfully interrupting the leaden delivery of whomever was speaking, and two waiters holding huge trays of margaritas entered the room. "Oh, Michael," Alfred drolly announced, "Your drink order is here." At every conference, our tradition was to start the day with Bloody Marys. Michael would be in the bar waiting for me: "Hi, Toots," he'd say by way of greeting, and we would proceed to gossip, make fun of each other, and fling insults at studious friends hurrying by on their way to sessions.

Yet beneath his affable exterior, there existed a serious scholar, devoted to his work and immersed in his field. He came out of the gate early and quickly established himself as one of the foremost authorities on the autobiographical writings of Mark Twain with the publication of *Mark Twain's Own Autobiography: Chapters from the North American Review* (1990), the only collection of autobiographical sketches that Mark Twain compiled for public evaluation; the second edition came out fortunately in 2010, a year before Michael's death. We worked together and coedited a special edition of the *Mark Twain Journal*, "Women in Mark Twain Biography" (1998), and coedited an edition of collected essays, *Constructing Mark Twain: New Directions in Scholarship* (2001). Michael also held a number of scholarly leadership positions, including president of the Northeast Modern Language

Association, president and founding member of the Mark Twain Circle of America, founding member of the editorial board of the *Mark Twain Annual*, president of the American Humor Studies Association, and editor of *Studies in American Humor*. These different roles were in multiple ways politically sensitive and required the grace of Princess Diana, the political acumen of LBJ, the organizational skills of a NASCAR pit crew, and the ripostes of Don Rickles—and Michael handled them all with his special mixture of élan, which included wearing his dogs-playing-poker tie and awful scarlet blazer (of dubious origin; he claimed it was linen), and I-don't-give-a-damn attitude.

While Michael had established his foremost scholarly credentials in his work with Twain's *Autobiography*, in my view he made another great contribution to the field in a talk he gave at Quarry Farm in 2001, subsequently published as one of the Quarry Farm Papers: "Samuel Clemens and Me: Class, Mothers, and the Trauma of Loss." In this piece Michael offered two innovative ways of talking about Twain and interpreting his work: The first shattered the academic third-person referent, and the second repositioned *Adventures of Huckleberry Finn* as a domestic novel.

As to the former, I had expected Michael to give his talk on Twain's writing, and his opening line, "I am going to start with me," made me involuntarily shudder as it appeared so self-referentially unseemly. This was before he really got going about his family. This sentence defied all of my training in New Criticism, where the "I," as well as any references to your subject's life, was carefully elided. By god this was literary criticism, deadly serious stuff! By 2001, I had, or so I thought, managed to divest myself of my New Critical baggage. After all, I had published my first biography/feminist/cultural study in 1993, which one appalled scholar in his or her anonymous-reader report referred to as a history manuscript, because it sure as hell was not English. Still, you could not find an "I" outside of the acknowledgments.

The academic scholarly default was third-person narrative, thank you very much, and the subject's life, and certainly yours, was inconsequential compared to the primacy of the text. Even when writing a biography, the writer was not to appear in the narrative. "This isn't about you," as the current phrase goes. The text you wrote—despite all the self you had invested in it—was to appear as if it had been delivered from on high, in the form of a granite tablet to be distributed among the faithful. This dryness was particularly characteristic of Twain scholarship, a quality Hamlin Hill called people out on in his commentary in 1974 on the state of Twain studies: "It is difficult to understand, but an author whose own frame of mind was always open to ironies, word plays, facetious turns of phrasing, and iconoclastic good fun has managed to attract some of the least pleasant scholarship and criticism in all American literary history."[2]

Yet, after getting over what I initially felt was Michael's solipsism and possibly his playfulness, I began to think, really think, about what he was trying to do. His opening sentence had a familiar ring to it and I quickly found a similar construction in Twain's writing: "You don't know about me without you have read a book by the name of *The Adventures of Tom Sawyer*; but that ain't no matter."[3] In beginning with the "I," my sense is that Michael was carefully positioning himself much as Twain had posited Huck as narrator. Michael, not unlike the character Huck, wanted you to know who he was and where he had come from and that it was a fallacy to pretend that his gender, race, sexual orientation, class, and background did not affect his thinking or seep into every line of his text: "And how we evaluate the lives we study—or, more importantly our own lives—lacks seriousness and resonance if we do not admit the primacy of home and class and the emotions that breathe in that mix."[4] In structuring his talk the way he did, Michael wanted us, to paraphrase T. S. Eliot, to see Twain's work from his eyes, not to merely view him from a fallacious objective distance.

Twain certainly was not kidding around when he cast Huck as the narrator of his tale. His was a shrewd and calculating choice. While Huck is a humorous character in many ways, and we frequently laugh at and with him, we also sympathize and empathize, too. Ultimately he is the most credible and serious person in the narrative, like it or not. And there were those who did not care for Huck at all, among them the good librarians of Concord, who were so appalled by Twain's choice of narrator—a narrator who plays hooky, smokes, and runs away, no less—that when the novel was first published, they banned it. What I finally figured out was that Michael, like Twain, was not kidding and that it was best to understand him as a trickster; he was the iconoclast Hamlin longed for.

In the same talk, Michael also permanently changed the way I thought about and read *Adventures of Huckleberry Finn*. Until then, my interpretation was a fairly traditional one: It was a novel "about" slavery, and Huck and Jim encounter a variety of situations along their backward journey down the river, most of them humorous in nature. That said, Twain's exploration of gender roles was interesting and important, particularly so in the Judith Loftus chapter, unless you wanted to write it off as slapstick, which would have been an obvious mistake. The ending was also widely considered bothersome, and I concurred with Leo Marx's opinion that by the end of his writing effort an exhausted Twain "nodded," so to speak; but while the ending was a farce, "the rest of the novel was not."[5]

Michael, though, interpreted the novel as a tale of domesticity lost. Huck's "adventure" more resembles a recurring nightmare, as this lost little boy searches for a home only to be continually thwarted. "Home," Michael wrote, "The loss of home. The quest for home. The legacy of mothers and the trauma of motherless children." We are not even through chapter 1, when Huck is living a "sivilized" domesticity with the Widow Douglas, who had taken him for her son, and Miss Watson, "a tolerable slim old maid," before he has a premonition of death, "a dog crying about somebody that was going to die."[6] In a tale bursting with episodes, dialect (Twain was careful to point out his facility in his explanatory note: "The shadings have not been done in a hap-hazard fashion, or by guess-work; but pains-takingly"[7]), and details, the demise of Huck's mother is never mentioned—she is a void, a silence, a loss too awful to mention. As Huck's Virgil, Jim escorts the boy down a river into an entropic world where each new adventure unleashes domestic scenes rotten and atavistic. The chatty and sometimes scolding Jim never mentions Huck's mother and spares him the sordid details of his father's murder, but he likely knows the awful story.

Huck is right on the money that misery and death are on their way, as Pap, one of the most terrifying figures in literature and who Twain makes an object of ridicule in order to cut the horrific tension, steals Huck away from the most stable existence he has ever known: "His hair was long and tangled and greasy, and hung down, and you could see his eyes shining through like he was behind vines. It was all black, no gray; so was his long mixed-up whiskers. There warn't no color in his face, where his face showed; it was white; not like another man's white, but a white to make a body sick, a white to make a body's flesh crawl—a tree-toad white, a fish-belly white."[8] Pap ferries his son across to the Illinois shore and decides to "stowe" him.

Michael describes Huck's role as narrator as focused "on the willful destruction of families," which the passage where Huck prepares to kill his father amply illustrates. "So he dozed off, pretty soon. By-the-by I got the old split-bottom chair and club up, as easy as I could, not to make any noise, and got down the gun. I slipped the ramrod down it to make sure it was loaded, and then I laid it across the turnip barrel, pointing towards Pap, and set down behind it to wait for him to stir. And how slow and still the time did drag along."[9] The mind-bending quality of Twain's genius is that he closes this unimaginably tragic novel with the delicate timing of the stand-up comedian and keeps you reading and laughing while standing drenched up to your neck in human misery.

Michael's presaging his reading of this particular passage with his own memory of an alcoholic father lent it a hard-survived insight that he was compelled to share with us. He knew where Huck was coming from: "An alcoholic father taught me the lesson of disappearing, of laying low and not saying anything because 'it would only make trouble, and wouldn't do no good.'" It should ultimately come as no surprise that by the end of the story Huck decides to "light out ahead of the Territory ahead of the rest, because Aunt Sally she's going to adopt me and sivilize me and I can't stand it. I been there before."[10] Huck's running away, in the end, was the only logical action from such a sensible soul. The only person he trusts has his existence threatened at every turn; Jim can no more protect him than that eunuch Judge Thatcher can.

In thinking about this in the midst of my grief, I recognize that Michael was always ahead of us in thinking about Twain and what meant most to him, and he kindly waited for the rest of us to catch up. I regret that I never had the chance to tell him this, but even if I had, I probably would not have said it out loud. Michael knew of my regard for him. After all, I usually paid for his drinks. My only solace in his untimely and heartbreaking departure is that maybe he has found the place that Huck longed for. I deliberately choose to believe this because I would not want to light out for any territory that did not have Michael waiting with a glass in hand to welcome me home.

LAURA SKANDERA TROMBLEY
—The Huntington Library

Mark Twain at Home

Introduction

"Momma, what is it all for?"
—Susy to Livy Clemens

MOST READERS HAVE no idea that Samuel Clemens was the father of four children or that he lived through the deaths of three of those children and his wife. Readers, in fact, rarely consider how all of that might finally (and perhaps irrevocably) have affected the way Clemens lived and the way he worked. Most readers also, I think, see Clemens as basically homeless—as one of the dispossessed who existed but did not live in the world, who faced none of the daily worries or joys that come with a household. On the contrary, children and home are important to our understanding of Samuel Clemens: Family is at the heart of his attraction to place and, more importantly, to his muse.

At the conclusion of *The Adventures of Tom Sawyer*, Samuel Clemens discovered Huckleberry Finn and recognized the child's sense of fear and urgency. Huck's voice resonates as he pleads with an insufferable and self-righteous Tom for entry into society (in the guise of Tom Sawyer's Gang). Tom reinforces the conventions of adult society, a society into which he has been welcomed by Judge Thatcher, who has assured Tom's adult career as soldier or lawyer. Acting as agent for the social norm, Tom attempts to bring a lapsed Huck back to the Widow Douglas' home. Huck left because he was increasingly uncomfortable with being "respectable." Tom says:

> "But, Huck, we can't let you into the gang if you ain't respectable, you know."
>
> Huck's joy was quenched.
>
> "Can't let me in, Tom? Didn't you let me go for a pirate?"

> "Yes, but that's different . . ."
>
> "Now, Tom, hain't you always been friendly to me? You wouldn't shet me out, would you, Tom? You wouldn't do that, now, would you, Tom?"
>
> "Huck, I wouldn't want to, and I don't want to—but what would people say? Why they'd say, 'Mph! Tom Sawyer's Gang! Pretty low characters in it!' They'd mean you, Huck. You wouldn't like that, and I wouldn't."[1]

Clemens needed two additional books to work through the implications of Huck's plea. In essence, *Tom Sawyer, The Prince and the Pauper,* and *Huckleberry Finn* tell one story—a story that follows a child through a maze of biological and social relationships in a quest for physical comfort and existential peace and calm. The movement through the three novels leads Clemens to an increasingly dark vision.

I did not read *Adventures of Huckleberry Finn* until I was twenty-seven years old and in my first semester of graduate school in a doctoral program. Mark Twain for me then was a new look into American literature and culture: My bachelor's and master's degrees emphasized British literature, and none of that coursework included any extended fiction by Mark Twain. The shift was fortuitous, and I have been reading and (at times) writing about assorted literary topics (mostly Mark Twain) ever since.

The topic of that first semester course in Mark Twain was "Mark Twain as Failed Artist." We examined, analyzed, and simply rushed through a substantial reading list, and we tried to consider whether Samuel Clemens had lived up to his creative potential or collapsed under the pressure and stress of a northern elite notion of art and whether his wife, Olivia, and his friend W. D. Howells had succeeded in keeping his tendency to burlesque under control. This, of course, was the approach begun by Van Wyck Brooks in *The Ordeal of Mark Twain*. For the most part, we decided that Clemens used his Mark Twain persona to broaden his humor and that, in the end, the literary persona was a valve through which Clemens was able to release the stresses. Creativity was a release, and Clemens was careful to bring out his best or worst under cover of his literary disguise, at least at first. We never, as I recall, dealt with the fact of Samuel Clemens' family life. It was mentioned, but it never became part of the approach to analyzing and unpacking Mark Twain's works.

That changed for me as I moved away from the usual course work and began to focus on my dissertation, a look at Clemens' process of creating his autobiography. Even later, when I edited *Mark Twain's Own Autobiography: The Chapters from the North American Review* (1990; rev. 2009), I began to realize that a good deal of Clemens' work building that text was an attempt to create a public monument to his family, and especially at that time, to Olivia and Susy. Clemens' wife and daughter are pivotal to the stories that he sought to preserve in his public presentation of his life and career, and that realization subsequently led me to think that, for Clemens, family was primary. I was not sure exactly how or what effect it had on his writing, but I was suspicious both of critics who dismissed Clemens' final years as a creative desert and of critics who ignored the echoes of family (or of families lost) in his major writing.

Some of my thinking about Clemens and family was sparked by my reading of nineteenth-century American women writers. In 1983 I was fortunate to be among a small class of graduate students who, under the guidance of Judith Fetterley, explored unavailable texts written by women during the mid- to late nineteenth century. The product of that course was Fetterley's anthology *Provisions: A Reader from 19th-Century American Women* (1985). For me, one of the most important books we read was Caroline Kirkland's *A New Home: Who'll Follow* (1839). Kirkland's sketches were a revelation, especially for a reader schooled to think in the easy categories and chronology of American realism and about Samuel Clemens' debt to a supremely and exclusively male line of humorists. Her use of the vernacular and, most importantly, her play between the male and female assumptions and visions of the frontier (which in 1839 was the Michigan woods) suggested a broader foundation for Clemens' humor, a foundation that seemed to me to have found new and fertile ground in the domestic situations of settlement life. In the end, Kirkland's collection of odd characters is tied together by mutual need, and their quirks and relations establish both the fact and feeling of community, which is the glue for her work. The same glue is at work in the fiction Sam Clemens created, though that embrace of a domestic-based community has rarely been recognized; instead, Clemens' settings have been characterized as locales given to a harvest of irony and satire, and his characters have been touted as supreme—and natural—individualists on the run from any hint of a female influence, from pressure to be "sivilized."

Although questions of belonging and the ways groups either embrace or exclude individuals inhabit a good deal of Clemens' early writing, much of that novice concern seems to focus on male exclusivity and, in terms of literary tradition, takes its cue from the tall tale's emphasis on male intimacy and the joke: Groups of insiders huddle around campfires or small stoves swapping tales (as in "Grandfather's Old Ram") and playing with the outsider or tenderfoot who becomes the butt of the long and involved joke (as in "The Celebrated Jumping Frog of Calaveras County"). Domesticity and a focus on community come to the fore in many of

Samuel Clemens' mature works, especially the novels composed and published from 1876 through 1894. More complicated definitions of community and more inclusive explorations of the relationship between individuals and the general community are central to Clemens' *The Adventures of Tom Sawyer, The Prince and the Pauper, Adventures of Huckleberry Finn, A Connecticut Yankee in King Arthur's Court*, and *The Tragedy of Pudd'nhead Wilson*. These mature works, in fact, depend on the various webs of domestic relations, especially as they begin to give shape and substance to Clemens' moral vision. My experience with Kirkland and the sharp critic Frances Whitcher taught me that Clemens' line of complex literary ancestors was decidedly maternal, which redirected my attention to how Clemens managed to blend humorist and moralist.

Clemens' moralism is intimately tied to the sentimental tradition that runs through the mid- to late nineteenth century. Clemens' realism is most often placed in opposition to the strained plot twists and more or less simplistic reliance on Christian ideology that holds sway in the bulk of popular mid-century fiction; however, unlike his Hartford neighbor Harriet Beecher Stowe and several of the dominant literary women of the time (including, most notably, Susan Warner), his novels are untidy and offer a less conventional Christianity as the guiding light of his various, and often orphan, characters. But that contrast is too easy and too shallow. Clemens' mid-career novels make it clear that he was deeply integrated into the Christian moral tradition, a tradition that shaped both his childhood, under the taut spiritual guidance of his mother, Jane Lampton Clemens, and his adulthood, especially, though not exclusively, under the influence of his wife, Olivia Langdon, and her family. His association with Livy's family and a variety of friends and acquaintances attuned to a collection of intellectual, spiritual, and social ideologies helped Clemens craft a mature use of the sentimental form. That constellation of influences, working on and affecting Clemens' own ideological shift during the early 1870s (in the years just after his marriage, in February 1870), came to a climax in *Adventures of Huckleberry Finn*.

In this scheme of sentimental fiction, Huck is defined not as the mid-twentieth-century poster child for American individualism but much more as a creature of the nineteenth century and its concern for the isolated and soul-sick orphan who seeks safety and redemption (both personal and spiritual) within a socially and spiritually acceptable family structure. Clemens embraces the sentimental tradition when he creates for his protagonist an overarching social context that is markedly and energetically unfriendly to the needs of a child at risk. Despite Widow Douglas' and Judge Thatcher's attempt to wrestle him from Pap's abuse, there is no heartfelt communal compassion for a child of poverty. Even after Huck escapes from Pap, he faces a constant physical threat from the adults he encounters along the river, a threat that is ironically more profound because of his pairing with Jim (a white boy seeming to aid a runaway slave would face consequences far worse than Huck's own naïve fear of being branded an abolitionist).

Combined with the physical threat, Huck faces a spiritual and existential crisis. While he has experience beyond his years in the domestic realm of power and violence, Huck is still stuck in a child's perspective that privileges the simple dichotomy between "right" and "wrong," a faulty morality that supports slavery and reinforces the rule of the powerful over the powerless. For Huck, there is no simple solution; there is no reliance on Christian epiphany or the potential for a Christian marriage to save this orphan from waste and destruction. Clemens uses Huck's predicament to underscore the tenuous status of the child and uses the mid-nineteenth-century understanding of childhood, which presents a conflict between the freedom afforded middle-class children and the various labors that were the lot of the poor, to frame Huck's continual slide between romantic notions of freedom and realistic constraints and limitations of class.

Central to all of this is the experience of loss. It is important to understand the breadth of loss within nineteenth-century families and its impact on children:

> But in a society in which half of all children lost a parent by the age of twenty, orphanhood was also a fact of life. As late as 1900, 20 to 30 percent of all children lost a parent by the age of fifteen. The number of orphaned and dependent children increased sharply in the late eighteenth century as a result of Revolutionary upheaval, increases of urban poverty, and cholera and yellow fever epidemics. A father's death almost inevitably thrust a working-class family into poverty, and the children were sent to live with relatives, indentured to another family, or placed temporarily in almshouses, where they lived along side criminals, paupers, prostitutes, and the insane. Some children were auctioned off to the lowest bidder through the public vendue system, sparing local communities the cost of supporting poor youth.[2]

Another way to save the community the cost of ministering to the youth was simply to cut them loose and to force the child to fend for himself or herself. Jacob Riis described the outcome of such abandonment both in *How the Other Half Lives* (1890) and *The Children of the Poor* (1892).

In *Huckleberry Finn* Clemens establishes Huck as a representative of those children who have suffered genuine and catastrophic loss (in the novel, that catastrophe is likely the loss of mother and siblings, a loss that propels Pap's anger and Huck's ambivalence). That backstory is important to our sense of the boy's character, and works, in the end, to complicate that character and his tale so that Clemens is able to challenge the usual construction of childhood, which posits the rural boy as free to embrace the romance of nature and to run from the constraints imposed by maternal rule. Here is the base interpretation for modern approaches to Huck's tale: He is seen as the natural child, the individual, on the run from domestic constraint. The reality, of course, is that Huck, for all intents and purposes an orphan, craves the stability and comfort of home. His options, though, are severely limited and are tainted by the presence of the fundamentalism of Miss Watson and the buffoonery of Uncle Silas.

Huck, however, is not the only character Clemens created that is deeply affected by the loss of family and driven by the impulse to find (or in some instances to replace or recreate) an integrated homelife. Nor is it the case that children are the only ones affected by loss. Each of the protagonists of Clemens' major fictions—Tom Sawyer, Huck Finn, Jim, Tom Canty, Edward VI, Hank Morgan, Roxy, Valet de Chambre, and Tom Driscoll—is shaped by his or her domestic situation, and each, as a result of a broken family and the emotional constriction caused by that loss, suffers a lack of genuine attachment. Most often, we read the stories that revolve around these characters and classify the tales according to setting or to some generic scheme (Mississippi and rural vs. England and urban; coming of age; adolescent; social commentary). We have, however, been slow to identify and explore their most basic similarities: the problem of home, the notion of filial relationship, the quest for comfort and family.

That quest is most often fed by a clear and abiding sense of loss. Critics and biographers have noted the absent father in many of Clemens' tales and have been quick to point to the death of John Marshall Clemens, in 1847, as an emotional focal point in Clemens' fiction. By all accounts, Clemens' father was reserved and emotionally distant from his family, and that, combined with his early death, which plunged the family into an ongoing financial crisis, created in Sam an emptiness that became manifest in his fiction. While this is a place to begin, it is not especially useful to look only to Clemens' youth for an entry into the fiction. There is a complex emotional turmoil at work in Clemens, a turmoil that has more to do with his reactions to events during his adult life than with quick and simplistic notions of the legacies of childhood. After all, while it is often the case that childhood trauma is replayed through adult attempts at expression, it is also true that adult worries and adult loss profoundly influence how individuals come to see the world, their ultimate place in it, and their power to challenge its ways. Adult emotions, while fed by memory, can produce a deep sense of responsibility for actions or events. The losses of our adult lives often vibrate more deeply as we try to navigate our way through the world. Adult feelings have their own depth and resonance separate even from the long-lasting effects of childhood's disappointments.

Above all, we must recognize that a study of deep feeling has been long missing in scholarship on Samuel Clemens, let alone on his literary alter ego Mark Twain. We focus on the how and the what of Clemens' life and career, but there are deeper questions: Why did an adult Samuel Clemens write so frequently about children forced to live on the margins, about children who, missing one or both parents, strive to make some life for themselves in the face of a hostile world? How is it that his most enduring characters, either child or adult, are those who push their way alone through the world? Is his work, dominated as it is with the wrecked lives of children or of adults who never seem to mature past a sense of loss and a companion narcissism, a celebration of male individualism (as it has often been presented and argued) or is it more accurately an exploration of the need for true sentiment and personal relationships in lives lived on the boundaries of community? Is his work, in fact, critical of selfishness and egocentricity? Finally and perhaps most radically, what effect does his own family experience, especially the experience of settling down and becoming a husband and a father (to three girls, no less), have on Samuel Clemens' writing and his notions of fiction as social statement?

Each of these questions opens a new horizon for our discussion of Samuel Clemens. The primary link among the questions is the overarching influence of domesticity, both as a literary tradition and as a life choice that, while constricting wanderlust and providing a stable and concentrated homelife, sparks a new and genuine sympathy for others, whether they be family, acquaintances, or strangers. Clemens' relationship with the dominant strain of literary domesticity needs to become part of the contemporary critical conversation. Driven as that conversation is by the shifting agendas of critics, it is important now to become more open to the possibilities offered by embedding Clemens within the dominant literary tradition of the nineteenth century. Such an interpretation is informed by feminist theory, which is clearly no longer outside mainstream literary study. Literary domesticity dominates the breadth of American fiction in the mid-1800s; it also offers insight into the development of American realism. The combination broadens our understanding of the symbiotic connections between writers and their cultural moments.

Samuel Clemens is deeply connected to this development. He did not emerge fully formed into the literary world but was shaped by literary movements and traditions, and he incorporated the dominant forms and perspectives of those traditions into his work. Over time, Clemens became a bright light on the American literary scene, but the strength of his popularity and success is based on his astute embrace of dominant forms while bringing to those forms an iconoclastic interest in the primacy of domestic emotional attachment.

There is also, though, the embrace of domesticity as a life choice, and Clemens, though always somewhat reticent about demonstrations of affection, gave himself completely to the ideals and practices of family and household. The genuineness of his conversion, which he described and boasted of in his courtship letters to Livy, has often been questioned; however, even his letters to Livy during their early days of friendship offer insights into his worry over and his absolute and practical need for the stability found only in the company of a woman able to love him. Clemens may have been raised to hold on to sentimental and Victorian values when it came to his search for a wife, but the practical effect of his bond with Livy was far from the pedestal: Livy became a helpmate, a strong and wily spouse who held Sam to his obligations and orchestrated their household to benefit his creative temperament. In short, once that courtship turned into betrothal and betrothal turned into marriage, Clemens embraced home without ambivalence. Huckleberry Finn's uncertainty about becoming "sivilized" was not Clemens' worry. Livy was Clemens' anchor; the family he and Livy created became and remained the bright light in Clemens' adult life. There is no better testament to Clemens' Promethean creativity than the connection between his growing family and his literary accomplishment.

That family/domestic aspect of Clemens' adult life has been too long dismissed or, worse, misinterpreted by critics who see his growing reliance on home and family as a mark of his weakness as an artist. For this batch of critics, whose ideas grow out of the initial judgments of Van Wyck Brooks, Clemens' homelife strangled his burgeoning talent and constricted his iconoclastic voice and creativity. Domesticity became the antithesis of "Mark Twain," perhaps even his demon, his opposition, and his villain; his literary heroes ran full throttle away from the domestic, and Samuel Clemens found only lukewarm and anemic inspiration in the home—both literally (signified by his characterization of Hartford as a dry well for his writing) and figuratively (as seen in the broken homes and domestic relationships that pepper his novels). This is simply wrong. Samuel Clemens worked most effectively when surrounded by family (whether in Hartford, Elmira, or on the road in Europe); his literary work was strongest when it dealt with the demands of home and family. Samuel Clemens could not have been the writer or the thinker he was, or have achieved his strong and vibrant voice, alone: His voice, in fact, was strongest when built in the chorus of family.

The last question—what effect his own family experience, especially of settling down and becoming a husband and a father, to three girls, no less, had on his writing and his notions of fiction as social statement—seems to me most compelling. The question drives our inquiry down a new path and presents us with a portrait of Sam Clemens that is unfamiliar to most critics, though it may be entirely unremarkable to lay readers who have long found Clemens' emotional life most compelling. In this view, Clemens' literary work can be seen through a stereoscope: One side offers a view of the professional writer who depends on his pen to support his family and to offer them opportunities material and cultural that will strengthen them individually and collectively; the other side offers a vision of Clemens' main themes and ideas and traces the change in both his topic and his tone as he comes to see the world not only as an object of humor and/or scorn but also as a place where his children will grow and, he hopes, prosper. Each view, though, is brought into sharp focus as Clemens becomes more deeply involved as a husband and a father. His sense of himself as a writer changes as he anchors himself in his family, and his subject matter emphasizes domestic concerns not only because of his childhood memories of his own broken family, which become less and less important, but also because he is mightily concerned with the reality of the world in which he and, more importantly, his children live. Ultimately, Clemens' agenda changes because of his children: He looks outward and is energized toward social criticism because he wants his daughters to be safe and their world more stable because it is more compassionate.

Seeing Clemens in this context requires a leap of faith and an assumption that a writer's work is affected by his (or her) household relationships. Neither step is natural to conventional literary criticism, which prizes textual and intertextual complexity. During my undergraduate and graduate training, I was taught to follow the precepts of New Criticism. The text was the primary focus, and it was the only genuine authority for any meaningful analysis. This taught me to prize the possibilities of rational analysis of myriad works and instructed me in the value of setting personal and emotionally sparked readings aside for the rigor of disinterested intellectual inquiry. I was excited with this new tool and pleased that I was able to gain insight and become adept at unpacking texts. And as I got better at analysis, I was able to don the robes of the critical priesthood. But deft and sophisticated analysis does not necessarily lead to the synthesis of ideas and experience. As I got older, and as I moved further along as a reader and a critic, I began to question my training and became skeptical of its antiseptic, rather cold, approach to reading. I began to see that writers (canonical or not) must be located within broad emotional contexts: the emotional context of both writer *and* critic. And I began to understand the symbiotic relation that sits at the heart of a critic's bond with the writer he or she chooses as a specialty. Critics do form almost familial bonds with writers; the more we know about a writer, the more we read the work in the context of their life (and our lives), and the stronger the emotional link between us gets. During the last fifteen years, while I have held to close reading as the primary strategy for literary interpretation, I began to see the potential for building meaning using a variety of strategies that highlight and enhance an emotional connection to the writer and his writing.

Most prominent among those strategies was reader response theory and the possibility it held for reorienting my understanding of how readers' experiences affect their relationships with texts. My own experiences brought my reading into new intellectual light and, more importantly, new emotional light. My reading became more meaningful as it became more personal. As I look back on it now, it was a small step from that embracing of the personal to exploring how a writer's experience influences his writing process and content. Yet I also can see the huge step I have taken away from my early training. My early work on Samuel Clemens and autobiography only enforced the idea that Clemens was especially affected by and made good creative use of his life. More than that, and far beyond the basic autobiographical references in his fiction (what has become known, for example, as the Matter of Hannibal), it became clear that Samuel Clemens' family life—his life with Livy, Langdon, Susy, Clara, and Jean—led him to a careful exploration of domesticity throughout his fiction. He was not, as I was taught, held completely by the glow of his Hannibal memories. He was, rather, intent on tying his own contemporary life to the variety of issues and concerns that encircled that life. In short, rather than run away from or dismiss domesticity, Samuel Clemens ran toward it and embraced its values and dynamics within his fiction.

As I became more intimate with Samuel Clemens' life, I found it less satisfying to keep my interpretive distance. As I reflected on the various losses in my own life, I found that those experiences only made my reading of Clemens' fiction and life more affective and, therefore, more effective. The more I was willing to invest in an emotion-based reading, the more I was able to bring Clemens to an audience of readers. As I have talked, taught, and written about that realization and its result, I have been able to trace Clemens' fascination (perhaps even compulsion) with domesticity and have come to see his fiction's foundation on a concern with family and on the intersections that lead his characters to embed themselves in the search for home. They do not run away from home unless they have to. And even when they take to the road, they are always and forever considering the paths that might lead them back.

That search, however, is not always grounded in nostalgia. Reading Clemens' interest in home as particularly nostalgic leads to a misapprehension of his involvement in the basic demands of his life and times.

1

Embracing Domesticity

The Adventures of Tom Sawyer

> I ain't doing my duty by that boy, and that's the Lord's truth, goodness knows. Spare the rod and spile the child, as the Good Book says. I'm a laying up sin and suffering for us both, know. He's full of the ol' Scratch, but laws-a-me! he's my own dead sister's boy, poor thing, and I ain't got the heart to lash him, somehow.
>
> —Mark Twain, *The Adventures of Tom Sawyer*

Samuel Langhorne Clemens and Olivia (Livy) Louise Langdon were married in the parlor of the Langdon family home in Elmira, New York, on February 2, 1870. On February 3, they were safely settled in Buffalo, New York, in a house that was a gift from Livy's father. Clemens was beginning what he assumed would be a long career as a newspaper editor and publisher; with help from his father-in-law, he had become part owner of the Buffalo *Express* in August 1869. That plan would be drastically changed within a year, when the Clemenses would leave Buffalo for Elmira and then Hartford, their pleasure with Buffalo ruined by the death of Livy's father, Jervis Langdon, in August 1870, as well as the premature birth of the Clemenses' son Langdon that November. The child remained sickly, and Livy's long bout with typhoid fever in February 1871 left her prostrate, already drained by the deaths of her father and a friend, Emma Nye, who had died in September 1870 while staying with the Clemenses.

In the days after the wedding, however, Clemens was aglow with the promise of his new life. After receiving a letter from Will Bowen, a childhood friend and companion from Clemens' Mississippi days, Clemens sat down with pen and paper on the afternoon of February 6. Through his late twenties in the West, Clemens had approached marriage in financial terms; however, in 1866 he had written (perhaps prophetically) to Bowen, "Marry be d——d. I am too old to marry. I am already 31. I have got gray hairs in my head. Women appear to like me, but d—n them, they don't *love* me."[1] Four years later, Clemens' relief and comfort are clear from the return address placed in the top right-hand corner of the letter:

> Sunday Afternoon,
> At Home, 472 Delaware Avenue,
> Buffalo Feb. 6, 1870

"At Home" suggests myriad emotions, grounded within notions of domestic safety, peace, and, for Clemens, a long-hoped-for stability.

Clemens' response to Bowen, addressed as "My First, & Oldest & Dearest Friend," teems with memories and sets the stage for a creative binge that just a few years ahead would spark into *The Adventures of Tom Sawyer*. The letter offers a clear contrast between past and present. It begins with an extended metaphor that suggests the passing of biblical time and a nostalgic glance back: "My heart goes out to you just the same as ever! Your letter has stirred me to the bottom. The fountains of the great deep are broken up & I have rained reminiscences for four & twenty hours. The old life has swept before me like a panorama; the old days have trooped by in their old glory, again; the old faces have looked out of the mists of the past; old footsteps have sounded in my listening ears; old hands have clasped mine, old voices have greeted me, & the songs I loved ages & ages ago have come wailing down the centuries! Heavens what eternities have swung their hoary cycles about us since those days were new!"[2] Clemens' sermonic cadence raises tension and adds a somber tone that underscores his seriousness. This is not a joke or even a prelude to a joke. It is a deliberate allusion to the time that has passed since childhood and childish things: The repetition of "old days" reinforces that separation and sets up the passing of "eternities . . . since those days were new!"

All of this is prelude to an extended list of reminiscences that conjure a past filled with childhood pranks and games (some of which, such as playing Robin Hood in shirt tails and with lathe swords, would find their way into his later fiction), Sunday school classes, and possible and actual drowning. Clemens' recollection, though, comes to an abrupt end with his mention of the days "since Laura Hawkins was my sweetheart." In a twist much like the one that will later close Hank Morgan's dream of Camelot, the allusion snaps Clemens (and Bowen) back to the present: "Hold! *That* rouses me out of my dream, & brings me violently back unto this day & this generation. For behold I have at this moment the only sweetheart I ever *loved*, & bless her old heart she is lying asleep upstairs in a bed that I sleep in every night, & for four whole days she has been *Mrs. Samuel L. Clemens*!"[3] Livy is Clemens' reality, and much like the contrast between present and past in the first section of the letter, he sets out to demonstrate her angelic qualities by calling up his own demonic habits: "Before the gentle majesty of her purity all evil things & evil ways & evil deeds stand abashed,—then surrender. Wherefore without effort, or struggle, or spoken exorcism, all the old vices and shameful habits that have possessed me these many many years, are falling away, one by one, & departing into the darkness. . . . She is the very most perfect gem of womankind that ever I saw in my life—& I will stand by that remark will I die."[4] And he did.

Livy brought stability into Clemens' vagabond life; his telling Bowen that he was "At Home" indicated that he was feeling at ease with his new life and was adapting to his role within a household. Clearly, with family comes a host of responsibilities and worries.

None of that would be lost on Clemens, especially in the later months of 1870 as he watched Livy care for her dying father, act as nurse for the terminally ill Emma Nye, and struggle through her pregnancy and Langdon's premature birth. It was, perhaps, a reminder of his mother's suffering: Though Sam was too young to recall the death of his brother Pleasant Hannibal Clemens, he would recall the deaths of siblings Margaret and Benjamin and could conjure the tortuous losses of his brother Henry Clemens and their father John Marshall Clemens. As Livy's father's health failed, Clemens wrote to Mary Mason Fairbanks: "There is no sound in the house—'the mourners go about' like spirits. Blinds are down & the gloom in the hearts of the household finds its type in the somberness of hall & chamber. . . . You understand what trouble we are in, & how the sunshine is gone out."[5] Domestic life held promise and pain, or perhaps more honestly the promise of pain.

Against that backdrop, Langdon Clemens was born on November 7, 1870. Amid the joy came a hint of future sorrow as Clemens wrote to his brother Orion, "Livy is very sick & I do not believe the baby will live five days."[6] Both survived the peril, and three days later Clemens turned down an offer to lecture in Philadelphia: "I have a strong desire to lecture again in Philadelphia . . . but piles & piles of money couldn't seduce me away from home this season! I'm a wet nurse, now, & I like it! We have got a baby & we don't want any more money nor any more glory either!"[7] Some five days later Clemens sent Susan Crane two pencil sketches of the baby sleeping in profile, along with his various measurements. Clemens was obviously a pleased and proud father.

So pleased was Clemens that he began to create dialogue to mark the relationship between him and his new son. In a letter to Charlie Langdon, Clemens reports a full conversation between parent and child, a conversation that begins with a comment about shoes and evolves into an exchange about language, specifically slang. At one point in the exchange, Langdon replies to his father, "I do not wish to have any words with you, father, but whenever you find that the nature of my conversation is not suited to your appetite, suppose you get up on your ear & take a walk 'round the block.'"[8] Langdon's comment echoes the language in Clemens' short sketch of his own linguistic battle with his father in "Wit-Inspirations of the 'Two-Year-Olds.'" The difference is that Langdon's insubordination is cherished and Clemens' was not, though even here there is a hint that humor (in this case a play on the allusion to the prophet Samuel's having to be called by God several times before responding) softens a father's wrath.

Yet amid his and Livy's pleasure with their new status and their child, there still hangs about them a sense of loss. For Livy, the loss of her father was especially acute as the first anniversary of Jervis Langdon's death approached. In a letter to her on August 8 or 9, 1871, Clemens responds to her anxiety and alludes to what must have been Livy's worry about what might happen should she die (the opening pages of the letter are not extant). He writes:

> Don't worry for us darling. If you are taken away, I will love the baby & have a jealous care over him. But let us hope & trust that both you & I shall tend him & watch over him till we are helped from our easy-chairs to the parlor to see his children married. Let us hope that way, sweetheart & try to trust that it will be so. In any case, you need not suffer any uneasiness about that influence you speak of. He shall never come under it. Better poison his body than his soul. Better make a corpse of him than a cur.[9]

While there is no way to reconstruct the "influence" mentioned here, it is clear that Clemens' intention is to assure Livy and to bring her comfort over the spiritual health of the boy.

Their move from Buffalo to Hartford, though fortuitous, put a heavy burden on the couple. Clemens spent a considerable time away from Olivia and their son on extended lecture tours during 1871 and 1872: He left on one such tour just after Olivia, again pregnant, and Langdon were settled in Hartford. Clemens' affection is clear in various letters that fall during his lecture tour as he reminds Livy to hug "the cubbie" or assures her of his deep affection: "Bless your heart, *I* appreciate the cubbie—& shall more & more as he develops & becomes vicious and interesting. To me he is a very very dear little rip."[10] In one of the few letters from Livy to Clemens during this period, dated November 22, 1871, she writes: "The baby is so sweet and dear. I know as he grows older you and he will love each other like *every thing*. What a wonderful thing love is, I do trust that we shall be a *thoroughly united loving family*—it certainly is the heaven here below—Youth in certain things you must teach me a 'don't care' spirit. . . . There is nothing that sooner ruins the happiness of a family than a worrying woman—Cubbie is very anxious to have you get home Sat. He hopes that you will not fail us on any account—"[11] The picture of the Clemenses as parents and as parenting partners suggest that both struggled with coming to terms with their new life as parents. Livy seems uncertain about Clemens' relationship with their son, an uncertainty that may grow out of Livy's own physical and emotional frailty magnified by the hovering presence of her lost father. Clemens himself struggles with fatherly attachment: He had no strong role model of fatherly affection in John Marshall Clemens, and the distractions of career and livelihood make it more difficult since he is often away from home. There is something frantic in his assurances to Livy, perhaps a result of his own ambivalence in the face of her maternal worry.

As 1871 passed, Clemens embraced a new beginning for his family and moved them out of Buffalo en route to setting their roots in Nook Farm, Hartford, Connecticut. Clemens' answer to Bowen, in fact, signals the beginning of a creative reappraisal. As Clemens wrote to Bowen, the success of *The Innocents Abroad* was becoming more apparent. And though he would stick with the *Express* and with writing for periodicals (especially the *Galaxy*) through 1870, by mid-1870 and through 1871, as he worked on his second big travel book, *Roughing It*, Clemens slowly came to a final decision to set aside the daily grind of newspaper work for what seemed a less constrained and more lucrative life as a writer of books. During this period he stepped more fully into the literary persona Mark Twain: The uses for that persona evolved away from the early convention of the pen name as a spark for humor and contrarian and burlesque commentary toward a serious and sharp social criticism. As Jeffrey Steinbrink has noted, "Most fundamentally, Mark

Twain had ceased for the most part to be an innocent himself and had become instead a commentator on innocence, frequently the innocence of his earlier life."[12] Though Clemens' writing is often embraced as a nostalgic look toward some idyllic past, it is more correct to see it as a way to offer clear and unabashed criticism of the contemporary world and its hard lessons. Clemens used the past as setting, but his intent is to bring readers face-to-face with the reality of his and their times; for example, *The Adventures of Tom Sawyer* is not about an antebellum village and past innocence but about Clemens' 1870s concern over community and the failure of moral instruction or, to put it another way, the loss of innocence. This all needs to be seen in the context of his life with Livy and their beginning to build their family.

Clemens irrevocably lost *his* innocence with the death of his son (his loss is reminiscent of Emerson's crisis at the death of his son Waldo and, in a different way, of Whitman's shock and reaction to the Civil War). Through early 1872 Clemens makes multiple references to Langdon's health and hardiness; however, there are also hints of a delayed development. On February 13, 1872, Clemens reports to Mary Mason Fairbanks that Langdon has not yet begun to walk (he is sixteen months old). Clemens passes this off humorously: "That is not backwardness of development physically, but precocity of development intellectually . . . since it is development of inherited indolence, acquired from his father." On April 22, Clemens mentions to Charles and Susan Warner that both Langdon and Susy are thriving, though "Langdon has no appetite. . . . His teeth don't come—& neither does his language."[13] In May Susy is still strong, but Langdon is weak after a bout of teething and a developing cough. That cough was a harbinger of a crisis, and after the Clemenses were back in Hartford (they spent some time in Elmira where Susy was baptized on May 26, 1872), Langdon's illness was diagnosed as diphtheria. He died on June 2. The parents were devastated. Lily Warner wrote to her husband: "Of course everyone thinks was a mercy that he is at rest—but his poor devoted mother is almost heart-broken. It is always so, I believe—those children that are the most delicate & need the most care—that everybody else wants to have die—are the most missed and mourned by their mothers. . . . Mr. Clemens was all tenderness but full of rejoicing for the baby—said he kept thinking it wasn't death for him but the beginning of life."[14] Livy was too weak to travel to Elmira for the burial; Clemens could not leave Livy alone. Langdon was buried after being laid out in the parlor of the Langdon home in Elmira, the same parlor in which the Clemenses were married. The one solace was Susy, and she became the light in their dark days. Absent parents are ubiquitous throughout Clemens' major fiction.

Could that awareness be driven by the experience of sending off his first born to face the grave alone?

As he approached the mid-1870s, Clemens used domestic life as both inspiration and script for a variety of short fiction. But he was careful to avoid a blunt biographical tie to the trauma of Langdon's death. Instead, Clemens often opted for the small insanities of mundane family life such as scenes of the family McWilliams. Clemens published three of the McWilliams sketches between 1875 and 1882: "Experience of the McWilliamses with Membranous Croup" (1875), "Mrs. McWilliams and the Lightening" (1880), and "The McWilliamses and the Burglar Alarm" (1882). The last piece is replicated in "Chapters from My Autobiography."[15] The sketches are slight and are best in presenting the off-hand banter between an exasperated husband and his rather high-strung wife. We find Clemens here exploiting and encouraging the conventional roles of husband and wife, mother and father, throughout the tales. He does have an ear for the language of the domestic sphere, yet he does nothing here that calls the stereotypical roles into question. The relationship of these sketches to the more substantial family-based novels and manuscripts is much like the relationship between Clemens' early frontier sketches and his later and more sophisticated use of the first-person narrative voice to break down notorious social custom.

However, at this time Clemens also takes aim at a more elemental family experience. "A True Story, Repeated Word for Word as I Heard It" (1874) derives its power from a supremely domestic situation: The story begins with a conventional picture of a well-to-do family, and especially its short-sighted and naïve patriarch, learning the story behind the external smiles of their servant. The tale is carefully controlled as the foolish narrator blunders into assumptions that he is able to hold only because of his social station and race: As an upper-class white man he assumes he can read the life of his black servant in her public actions. His description of "Aunt Rachel" is rife with false assumptions and shallow understanding: "She was a cheerful, hearty soul, and it was no more trouble for her to laugh than it is for a bird to sing. . . . She was being chaffed without mercy, and was enjoying it." In his ease and comfort, he asks, "Aunt Rachel, how is it that you've lived sixty years and never had any trouble?" This becomes a teachable moment, and Aunt Rachel presents to him a tale that underscores Paul Laurence Dunbar's "We Wear the Mask."

What follows is a harrowing tale of loss and the joy of the redeemed as Aunt Rachel schools her foolish employer about the realities of slavery and prejudice and especially about his own privilege and lack of sympathy. The tale is meant to introduce the narrator to pain and loss, a pain that he is too quick to assume has been missing in a life of a black woman. As Rachel begins, she sets out her own humanity in relation to the narrator's by insisting that her husband was "jist as kind as you is to yo' own wife" and that they loved their children "jist the same as you loves yo' chil'en." She reinforces that last comparison by asserting, "Dey was black, but de Lord can't make no chil'en so black but what dey mother loves 'em an' wouldn't give 'em up, not for anything dat's in dis whole world." The hook within the tale is Rachel's rant, "I want you niggers to understan' dat I wa'nt bawn in de mash to be fool' by trash! I's one o' de ole Blue Hen's Chickens, I is!"[16] It is a call learned from her mother, and it is that call that prompts her son (now an adult) to realize he is in the presence of his lost mother. Those few comments emphasize the domestic and maternal. The tale itself revolves around the trauma of loss, for even when Rachel finds her lost Henry at the end, she is still without her husband and six of her children.

For Clemens, the tale grows out of a combination of two memories: The lost son here is Henry, reminiscent of Clemens' younger brother who was killed in the explosion of the steamboat *Pennsylvania* in 1858. On June 18, 1858, Clemens, still a cub riverboat pilot, held vigil as his younger brother slipped into death. He wrote to their sister: "Long before this reaches you, my poor Henry—my darling, my pride, my glory, my *all*, will have finished his blameless career, and the light of my life will have gone out in utter darkness. . . . The horrors of three days have swept over me—they have blasted my youth and left me an old man before my time."[17] In 1874, that vigil, along with those he kept for Jervis Langdon, Emma Nye, and, perhaps most affecting, Langdon and the time he sat to nurse Livy in her grief, coalesce into the voice of the black mother who suffers the loss of home and children. It is, in fact, all of a piece. Langdon's loss was still a fresh wound, and if we consider its importance by how often Clemens does *not* mention it (similar to Huck Finn's silence about the death of Buck Grangerford), we begin to see how Clemens' stories pivot on the unmentionable wound. Rachel's missing son is reunited with his grieving mother, something that was not possible for the Clemenses. "A True Story," then, is a conjure story that brings back the dead and presents the story of that resurrection for a larger social purpose.

Recollection seasoned with social purpose leads to Clemens' decision to focus on novel writing. By 1874 Clemens had already been working away at *The Adventures of Tom Sawyer* for roughly two years (bits and incidents that find their way into the novel appear in his notebooks as early as 1866). The book's thematic pedigree links it to the variety of Sunday School literature that was popular at the time, especially a relation to Thomas Bailey Aldrich's *The Story of a Bad Boy* (1869). If Tom were to describe his own "rebellion" he might echo the words of Aldrich's hero: "I call my story the story of a bad boy, partly to distinguish myself from those faultless young gentlemen who generally figure in narratives of this kind, and partly because I really was *not* a cherub. I may truthfully say I was an amiable, impulsive lad, blessed with fine digestive powers, and no hypocrite. . . . In short, I was a real human boy . . . and no more like the impossible boy in the story-book than a sound orange is like one that has been sucked dry."[18] Tom is kin to earlier "bad" boys cast in Clemens' parodies of morality stories: "Advice for Good Little Boys," "Advice for Good Little Girls," "The Christmas Fireside: The Story of the Bad Little Boy That Bore a Charmed Life" (1865), and "The Story of the Good Little Boy Who Did Not Prosper" (1870). The pranks and small upsets that Tom instigates ally him with those boys who are more interested in poking at authority than in challenging social custom.

The focus for authority in the novel is the home and the institutions that revolve around and support the domestic sphere, the church, and the school. The tale revolves around the domestic center: the household of Aunt Polly. Polly, the sister of Tom's dead mother, has taken in her sister's children: The extended family group includes Tom's half-brother Sid and his cousin Mary (who may be Polly's daughter; her familial tie is never clarified, but it's unlikely that Mary is a Sawyer). Both take their lumps as part of Tom's bristling against rules, especially Sid. In his autobiography, Clemens identifies Henry Clemens as the model for Sid, which by allusion if not explicit statement links young Sam to Tom and Jane Lampton Clemens to Polly:

> My mother had a good deal of trouble with me, but I think she enjoyed it. She had none at all with my brother Henry. . . . I think that the unbroken monotony of his goodness and truthfulness and obedience would have been a burden to her but for the relief and variety which I furnished in the other direction. I was a tonic. I was valuable to her. I never thought of it before, but now I see it. I never knew Henry to do a vicious thing toward me, or toward any one else—but he frequently did righteous ones that cost me heavily. It was his duty to report me, when I needed reporting and neglected to do it myself, and he was very faithful in discharging his duty. He is "Sid" in "Tom Sawyer." But Sid was not Henry. Henry was a very much finer and better boy than ever Sid was.[19]

The notion that Clemens suffered from Henry's righteousness reinforces the battle lines between domestic order and chaos. But, truth be told, neither Sam nor

Tom is intent on destroying the fabric of the family: As a child Clemens embraced the overarching value of sympathy as necessary for the survival of the family in the face of crises economic and social. After the unexpected death of his father, he goes willingly to an apprenticeship that will help him learn a trade and that will, further, make it possible for him to serve his older brother as Orion opens and closes a variety of newspaper or printing establishments. Even his later decision to learn the river is a way for him both to find his own path and to offer aid to his mother and siblings.

In the novel, the issue becomes whether Tom will manage to cultivate a future in the shallow soil of St. Petersburg society. There is no question, however, whether that future will depend on his embrace of the domestic and his giving himself to a conventional male role. True to Clemens' interest in the results of seemingly transgressive behavior (in tweaking social norms while never truly challenging the basic values of the community), Tom ends up improving both his economic standing within the community and assuring his own comfortable future by impressing the influential community member Judge Thatcher (a strategy related to the rags to riches stories of Horatio Alger). The "bad" that he does never places him completely outside or at odds with society. Even in *Huckleberry Finn* when Tom acts against fundamental notions of human sympathy, which he does by keeping quiet about Jim's freedom while subjecting the slave to a host of indignities, Tom is always true to community moral and ethical standards: If sin is defined as taking genuine steps to undermine or to question the community's values, then Tom cannot be said to be a sinner. Even his violation of notions of human compassion is negated by the community's stern disregard of real sympathy in its embrace of prejudice and slavery.

Clemens approaches this question by placing Tom in situations in which he is faced with breaching the social/community contract. Later, in *Huckleberry Finn*, Clemens will create a story that places his protagonist squarely in the middle of a plot that calls into question a whole community's allegiance to compassion and mercy—that will be the fulcrum of the novel and will set the stage for Huck's running away when he realizes that there is no chance of safety while he is in Pap's control, a control that is both allowed by St. Petersburg and endorsed by adult law. In this earlier novel, however, Clemens is at the beginning of his own exploration of the relationship of the child to the adult world of social custom and legal precedent and has not yet come to the point where his children find themselves in full exile. Tom is never under stresses similar to those that overcome Huck; instead, he remains connected to the fabric of the town and considers himself to be one of its central actors. He finds his way to reinforce his central role as he decides to shift his loyalty from a child's world to the adult system of justice and social order. In one telling moment, for example, Tom must weigh the value of his personal oath to Huck Finn against the adult rule of law. When a terrible storm lights up his conscience at the end of chapter 22, Tom assesses his place within and duty to the community's law: "And that night there came a terrific storm, with driving rain, awful claps of thunder, and blinding sheets of lightening. He covered his head with the bedclothes and waited in a horror of suspense for his doom; for he had not the shadow of a doubt that all this hubbub was about him. He believed he had taxed the forebearance of the powers above to the extremity of endurance and that this was the result. It might have seemed to him a waste of pomp and ammunition to kill a bug with a battery of artillery, but there seemed nothing incongruous about the getting up of such an expensive thunderstorm as this to know the turf from under an insect like himself" (179). It seems as if Jonathan Edwards' God has focused His power to get the boy to conform to the legal and moral needs of the accused, and Tom takes the hint. After Tom and Huck swear themselves to secrecy yet again, a precaution in the midst of the community's uproar about the trial of Muff Potter for the murder of Doc Robinson, they go to visit the jailed Potter. In a speech that mixes melodrama with a temperance lecture, Potter unwittingly plays on the boys' consciences:

> You've been mighty good to me, boys—better'n anybody else in this town. And I don't forget it, I don't. Often I says to myself, says I, "I used to mend all the boys' kites and things, and show 'em where the good fishin' places was, and befriend 'em what I could, and now they've all forgot old Muff when he's in trouble; but Tom don't, and Huck don't—*they* don't forget him," says I, "and I don't forget them." Well, boys, I done an awful thing—drunk and crazy at the time—that's the only way I account for it—and now I got to swing for it, and it's right. Right, and *best*, too, I reckon—hope so, anyway. Well, we won't talk about that. I don't want to make *you* feel bad, you've befriended me. But I want to say, is, don't *you* ever get drunk—then you won't ever get here. Stand a little furder west—so—that's it; it's a prime comfort to see faces that's friendly when a body's in such a muck of trouble, and there don't none come here but yourn. Good friendly faces—good friendly faces. Git up on one another's backs and let me touch 'em. That's it. Shake hands—yourn'll come through the bars, but mine's too big. Little hands, and weak—but they've helped Muff Potter a power, and they'd help him more if they could. (183–84)

The speech is a powerful influence on the boys' sense of right, which here is based on their personal relationship to the doomed Potter. Muff's comments focus on a history of personal kindnesses, and it is that history, rather than a general sense of legal or social justice, that touches Tom's and Huck's consciences (the conversation is a rehearsal for the later review of Jim's kindnesses that influence Huck to attempt to steal Jim out of slavery in chapter 31 in *Huckleberry Finn*). Huck is torn but will not breach the oath that he has made with Tom; however, Tom decides after the twin presentiments sparked by the storm and Muff's speech to abandon the oath of silence that he crafted with Huck. He leaves behind the games of childhood to participate fully in the adult community by arranging with the prosecutor to testify in court; he embraces adult social and spiritual norms rather than the values of childhood friendship.

Huck is devastated by the turnabout. He is, of course, worried that he will pay a price for Tom's honor. More importantly, he has had another taste of abandonment for adult principles of justice and possibly fame: "Since Tom's harassed conscience had managed to drive him to the lawyer's house by night and wring a dread tale from lips that had been sealed with the dismalest and most formidable of oaths, Huck's confidence in the human race was well nigh obliterated" (190). Ironically perhaps, Tom's abandoning the oath makes it easier for the uninitiated Huck later to leave behind his allegiance to Tom's scheme for treasure to protect the Widow Douglas from Injun Joe's physical threat. Notice, however, Tom's deliberate choice leads to accolades and (indirectly) to riches; Huck turns away from the possibility of riches to act out of a sense of obligation and humanity. Perhaps because of his low status and marginal existence, as well as his experience with an alcohol-affected household, he is the one who absorbs Muff Potter's lecture and turns more emphatically toward an act of mercy without any intention of milking profit from it.

Clearly one of Tom's primary motivations is to establish and then strengthen his personal standing within the community (child and adult). At first, his self-centeredness echoes that of a typical adolescent boy who strives to be seen: Attention is its own reward. Early in the novel, he lays down under Becky Thatcher's window and pines away for her attention, attention that is always most emphatic when sparked by an early and untimely death: "Then he laid himself upon his back, with his hands clasped upon his breast, and holding his poor wilted flower. And thus he would die—out in the cold world, with no shelter over his homeless head, no friendly hand to wipe the death damps from his brow, no loving face to bend pityingly over him when the great agony came. And thus *she* would see him when she looked out upon the glad morning, and oh! would she drop one little tear upon his poor, lifeless form, would she heave one little sigh to see a bright young life so rudely blighted, so untimely cut down?" (40). Such sentiments work through the novel and inform Tom's later embrace and manipulation of the town's grief when the boys are thought to have drowned. In chapter 15, Tom has the opportunity to hear his aunt's piteous mourning for her lost child. Polly opines, "He warn't so bad, so to say—only mischeevous. Only just giddy, and harem-scarum, you know. He warn't any more responsible than a colt. *He* never meant any harm, and he was the best-hearted boy that ever was" (129). Her tears almost drive Tom out of hiding and into her arms. Almost. They do prompt him to leave a note for her, which is in itself a bow to the filial relation that is at the center of the domestic relationship. Tom's motives become more complex here as he yearns for fame but begins to understand that such attention is only possible within the domestic sphere.

The boys' return to the living, while important in a plot driven by Tom's quest for adventure, reunites the lost with their families. That is, Tom and Joe are taken up with joy as the prodigal sons they are. The one true outsider is Huck. He has no one to welcome him home, no one to mark his return from the dead, which by implication suggests that he is expendable and lost to the world. While awaiting Tom's return to Jackson Island, Huck, who has learned from Tom's slight of their earlier oath, is ready to consider that Tom has abandoned the boys. Yet, later during the celebration of their resurrection, Tom seeks to bring Huck into the domestic sphere and pleads for someone to embrace the lost child: "Aunt Polly, it ain't fair. Somebody's got to be glad to see Huck." Polly is quick to pick up on the slight: "And so they shall. *I'm* glad to see him, poor motherless thing!" (147). Huck is mortified with the attention. He is not Tom. He is also suffering from the reminder of his orphan status and reacts with the knowledge that no stranger can replace his dead mother. He remains loyal to her memory, even if that loyalty results in compounding his aloneness and exile.

Tom's quest to belong comes to depend on a relationship with Aunt Polly and, through her, with the whole of the adult community. His first understanding of responsibility develops within the tight frame of the household, and while he bristles and bucks against the tight reins of domesticity, he ultimately comes to embrace the ideas of self and social control. He is introduced to the reader as he hustles away from Aunt Polly's reach, and subsequent episodes reinforce his (at least mild) rebellion against domestic order: He undermines Polly's notion of disciplined work by manipulating other boys to whitewash the fence, he joins the rest of the congregation in finding distraction and entertainment during Sunday church services, and he causes a stir in school by standing up to the schoolmaster.

Tom, however, becomes much more prone to convention and custom: He reinforces gender roles by taking steps to protect Becky Thatcher from the overly zealous punishment of the schoolmaster, he bows to a sense of responsibility and mercy when he leaves Polly a note to assure her that he is safe when off pirating, and ultimately he performs in the best romantic-swashbuckling tradition as he shields Becky from Joe while they are lost in the cave. This last action results in his transferring his allegiance to adult custom and convention, for which he is rewarded by Judge Thatcher, who plans to assure Tom's future as a lawyer or military man, the two male roles that most represent the status quo within any adult community —law and its enforcement and protection. Above all, Tom is careful to keep up appearances.

The Adventures of Tom Sawyer, then, rather than being the story of a social outrider and of the potential for chaos when social and specifically domestic rules are stripped away, presents a story of a precocious child who remains true to the basic community values and who, in the end, embraces and enforces domesticity. This is not a portent of revolution. If anything, Tom holds the center of the tale firmly together. He exerts a centripetal force: He is reined in and reins in others (Huck especially) because of his notion of social and community relation and the lessons of Aunt Polly, who, for all her uncertainty and bluster, stands as the lone representative of family in her nephew's small world. Clemens understood the strength and value of domestic relations, and he fashions a novel that reminds adult readers of their necessary and inevitable mature selves. He deliberately alludes to this in his short preface: "Although my book is intended mainly for the entertainment of boys and girls, I hope it will not be shunned by men and women on that account, for part of my plan has been to pleasantly remind adults of what they once were themselves, and of how they felt and thought and talked, and what queer enterprises they sometimes engaged in" (ix).

Importantly, Clemens ties his story most emphatically to men and women. William Dean Howells convinced Clemens that the novel should be aimed at an audience of children: "I finished reading Tom Sawyer a week ago, sitting up till one A.M. to get to the end, simply because it was impossible to leave off. It's altogether the best boy's story I ever read. It will be an immense success. But I think you ought to treat it explicitly *as* a boy's story. Grown-ups will enjoy it as much if you do; and if you should put it forth as a study of a boy's character from the grown-up point of view, you'd give the wrong key to it. . . . The adventures are enchanting. I wish *I* had been on that island. The treasure-hunting, the loss in the cave—it's all exciting and splendid."[20] Clemens never really reconciled himself to that adjustment; instead, he worked deliberately to create a story that relied on a sense of nostalgia but also on an adult sense of what makes or breaks a community.

While it was his own remembrance that prompted the preface's emphasis on the adult experience of nostalgia, more and more Clemens turned away from the past as subject and toward a strong interest in the present. Readers have been too quick to pigeonhole Clemens' novel as a work that looks back into some kind of ideal childhood experience. Admittedly, the early chapters of the novel are tied to an adult's fond recollection of the ways of childhood: Tom's scrapes with Aunt Polly, his ability to lead other children in imaginative play and the definition of work, and his early experience of infatuation all reconstitute the life of a small-town boy on the cusp of adolescence. But there is also criticism of the adult world, with its interest in "showing off" at the Sunday School exercise, its deadening of religious faith that turns Sunday worship into a sideshow, its practice of physical and emotional violence to discipline the schoolhouse, and its failure to recognize and inability to punish evil. The adult community also is content to avert its eyes from the needy and the plight of a child marginalized by his poverty and left alone by a negligent and violent father. Huckleberry Finn, who begins the novel as a supporting character to Tom's self-absorbed shenanigans, by the end becomes a focal point for a wholly different story, a story that is not primed by Mississippi reminiscence but by Clemens' adult experience of the world and his concern with the social ostracism of children who are not connected or who have no recourse to patronage by the elect.

Throughout the novel, Huck remains an outsider. Even though he is embraced by Polly when he arrives safe with Tom and Joe fresh from their drowning, he finds it difficult to accept Polly's ministrations. Later, he risks his own life both physically, by opening himself to Joe's revenge, and, mostly likely, emotionally, by reaching for help from people who may slight and ignore him once again. Though he runs for help to protect the Widow and though she is determined to "adopt" him into her household, Huck remains aloof from foster care and rebels against the order and behavior that is expected by all members of "civilized" society. Huck's steps away from St. Petersburg are intercepted by Tom, who has by this time become a faithful enforcer of community standards. He browbeats Huck into returning to the Widow Douglas:

> "Lookyhere, Huck, being rich ain't going to keep me back from turning robber."
>
> "No! Oh, good licks, are you in real dead-wood earnest, Tom?"

> "Just as head earnest as I'm sitting here. But Huck, we can't let you into the gang if you ain't respectable, you know."
>
> Huck's joy was quenched.
>
> "Can't let me in. Tom? Didn't you let me go for a pirate?"
>
> "Yes, but that's different. A robber is more high-toned than what a pirate is—as a general thing. In most countries they're awful high up in the nobility—dukes and such."
>
> "Now Tom, hain't you always been friendly to me? You wouldn't shet me out, would you, Tom? You wouldn't do that, now, would you, Tom?"
>
> "Huck, I wouldn't want to, and I *don't* want to—but what would people say? Why they'd say, 'Mph! Tom Sawyer's Gang! pretty low characters in it!' They'd mean you, Huck. You wouldn't like that, and I wouldn't." (272)

The cycle is complete. Just as Tom taught Huck a first lesson in the mature relation of an individual to lawful society by trashing their blood oath to testify in court, at the end of the tale Tom stands both as enforcer and as judge as he intimidates and pressures Huck to conform. Tom knows that Huck's one worry is whether he will ever truly belong anywhere, and he uses Huck's insecurity and need to push him to accept society's demands. In the end, if Huck wants to have friends, if he wants to remain among the small and exclusive group that forms Tom Sawyer's Gang (itself an expression of Tom's social control), he must acquiesce to the demands of proper custom and return (cowed and chastised) to the Widow's home. Tom Sawyer, for all intents and purposes, in the end forces Huckleberry Finn to return to the control of the Widow Douglas. In a most profound sense, he pushes Huck, who by the way still has a biological father, to turn away from his family and the memory of his mother to accept foster care. It is not a happy result for Huck. But that, in the end, does not matter. It is what Tom and the Widow and the Judge and the community want.

That ending is a good distance away from the idyll (even if it is a rough idyll) in the early chapters and suggests that Clemens' primary interest in the children had shifted away from the bound-to-succeed Tom to the fated-to-destruction Huck. While the tale might have begun with Clemens' memories of childhood friends and acquaintances, there is a great deal more at work here than the memories of the Blankenship family. In "Chapters from My Autobiography" Clemens' memory vacillates as he identifies first Frank Finn and then Tom Blankenship as the source for Huck;[21] however, his late recollection is tinged with the description of Huck from *Tom Sawyer*:

> He was ignorant, unwashed, insufficiently fed; but he had as good a heart as ever any boy had. His liberties were totally unrestricted. He was the only really independent person—boy or man—in the community, and by consequence he was tranquilly and continuously happy, and was envied by all the rest of us. We liked him; we enjoyed his society. And as his society was forbidden us by our parents, the prohibition trebled and quadrupled its value, and therefore we sought and got more of his society than of any other boy's. I heard, four years ago, that he was Justice of the Peace in a remote village in the State of [Montana], and was a good citizen and was greatly respected."[22]

The description is more in keeping with the introduction of Huck in chapter 6 of *Tom Sawyer* than with the narrative line at the end of the novel. And the possibility of social redemption (signified by the irony of becoming a justice of the peace) is certainly far from the reality of the tale Huck will tell in his own book. Clemens seems to have given himself over to the romantic vision of his realistic character. Some years earlier, in "Villagers of 1840–3," a series of notes on Hannibal composed around 1897, Clemens recalled the Blankenships: "The parents paupers and drunkards; the girls charged with prostitution—not proven. Tom, a kindly young heathen. Bence, a fisherman. These children were never sent to school or church. Played out and disappeared."[23] The final comment here—"Played out and disappeared"—seems much more in line with the reality of lighting out for the territories, the absence of responsible compassion in a community, and the inability of an abused boy to exhibit trust.

Clemens intimates the occurrence of domestic violence in *Tom Sawyer*, with Huck at one point responding to Tom's plan for marriage by saying, "Well, that's the foolishest thing you could do. Look at pap and my mother. Fight! Why, they used to fight all the time. I remember, mighty well." In the same conversation, Huck admits to a grave lack of financial planning by dreaming of spending his part of the pirate treasure on daily pie and soda, a plan sparked by the greed of Pap: "Pap would come back to thish-yer town some day and get his claws on it if I didn't hurry up, and I tell you he'd clean it out pretty quick" (177). But these slant mentions are relatively obscure within the whole of the tale and still serve to enhance Tom's stature. What caused Clemens to shift his interest at the end of *Tom Sawyer* to the more realistic and problematic version of Huck's history? And what might be the transformative moment for a character (and a writer) who enters into a dark and forbidding tale of marginal lives?

As Clemens worked toward the finish of *Tom Sawyer*, New York and its environs faced a turning point in the social politics of child welfare. During April 1876, the case of nine-year-old Mary Ellen Wilson, a child who was kept a prisoner by her foster mother and used daily as a whipping post, came to light and generated the first meaningful reform of child protection. Clemens no doubt read about the case in the New York newspapers; the court proceedings were widely reported in the *New York Times*, the *New York Herald*, the New York *Evening Post*, and the *New York Tribune*. The papers ran headlined stories about the case during April 1874, as well as updates through June and into December. The coverage of April 10 through 14 was especially thick with descriptions of the child just after her rescue that lingered on her physical bruises and her account of her living conditions and beatings. The facts of the case must have jogged Clemens' childhood memories of Hannibal's Blankenships as well as pricked his sensitivity to the small voices that echoed through the Clemenses' Farmington Avenue house in Hartford (Susy's at four and Clara's at two). The combination and the contrast would have been a potent mixture.

Mary Wilson began the journey into abuse after the death of her father, Thomas Wilson, killed in service of the Union during the Civil War; her mother, Frances (Connor) Wilson, lived for a while on his soldier's pension, but she eventually handed over her daughter (along with a portion of the pension) to another woman when she could no longer support the child. Mary Score took the child in to supplement her family's income. This arrangement might be considered part of the "child farming" that was common among the working class and working poor in New York at the time, though there is no evidence that either Fanny Wilson or Mary Score intended any harm to come to the girl. In July 1865 Score handed the girl over to the Department of Public Charities and Corrections after the payments from Fanny Wilson stopped (no reason for the halt of the payments was ever discovered): On July 10, 1865, Mary Ellen Wilson was placed in one of the children's wards at Blackwell's (now Roosevelt) Island. According to Eric Shelman and Stephen Lazoritz, "Mary Ellen was one of the fortunate survivors of New York orphanages, which experienced average death rates of 85 percent during this period of rampant disease and unsanitary conditions."[24]

The child was "adopted" from Blackwell's on January 2, 1866, by Mary and Thomas McCormack, who were able to claim the child with no evidence of filial connection but with a mere promise to care for her physically and to some small extent spiritually. (Thomas asserted that Mary Ellen was his illegitimate child, born after an affair with the child's mother, though no evidence has ever been found to support his claim). The document the McCormacks signed on February 13, 1866, was an agreement of indenture, which placed Mary Ellen in their home until she was eighteen years old. After Thomas' death, Mary McCormack married Francis Connolly and the family moved to West 41st Street.

Young Mary Ellen was one more orphan in one more "home" until April 9, 1874, when the beaten, isolated, and stunted child was rescued by agents of Henry Bergh, president of the New York Society for the Prevention of Cruelty to Animals (NYSPCA), and New York City police officers at the urging of Etta Angell Wheeler, a Methodist caseworker. The case, argued by Elbridge Gerry, the lawyer for Bergh's NYSPCA, precipitated the founding of the New York Society for the Prevention of Cruelty to Children. Gerry's insight was to claim that the long-ignored section 65 of the Habeas Corpus Act gave the State the duty to invade a home to wrest a child from a guardian when the child faced certain injury from abuse or neglect. Gerry and Bergh had collaborated in a similar case in 1871 when a young child, Emily Thompson, was removed from her home because of abuse; the judge in the case ultimately returned the child to the home because she was unwilling to be separated from the woman she had come to see as her mother and because the child presumably had no living relatives; there were also numerous calls for Bergh to broaden his concern to children in the New York papers during the late 1860s and early 1870s. Gerry's argument carried in 1874, after an extended set of hearings and testimony from a variety of individuals either directly or indirectly connected with Mary Ellen Wilson's situation.

Along with Clemens' childhood experiences with various families who were broken by early deaths (his own being one of them), it is also likely that he knew and was sensitive to the history of his sister-in-law Susan Crane. Born Susan Dean, her family was disrupted by the early deaths of both parents. Her mother died in 1837, when Susan was nineteen months old; her father died in 1840. There were several children, and Susan remained in touch with her older brother Stephen throughout his life. Taken into the Langdon home, Susan was nine years old when Olivia was born in 1845. While certainly not a tale of woe and abuse, Susan's situation in the Langdon home was an example of the success possible when a family steps in on behalf of a lost and at-risk child. Clemens no doubt knew of Susan's and the Langdons' story: One can only wonder whether in Mary Wilson's tale there wasn't some prodding of the Clemenses' collective memory or at least some reminder of the plight of the orphan facing the world. It also lends a personal history to what had become in the 1870s a dire situation for New York City's children. In the case of Ellen Wilson, Mary Webb, the police matron in charge of children brought in by the police, testified, "In warm weather we average 300 a month. In the month of May we have had 400."[25] On April 14, 1874, the *New York Times* and the *New York Tribune* reported that five hundred children had passed through the Department of Charities during the previous year.

The newspaper reporter present when Mary Ellen Wilson was brought into court was Jacob Riis, who later went on to write *How the Other Half Lives* (1890) and *The Children of the Poor* (1892), influential exposés on tenement life and on the rampant poverty and violence visited on the children in New York City. In *The Children of the Poor*, Riis reconstructed the scene of the child's introduction in court and the resulting furor: "The appearance of the starved, half-naked, and bruised child when it was brought into court wrapped in a horse-blanket caused a sensation that stirred the public conscience to its very depths."[26] That memory is borne out by contemporary coverage of the trial in the New York press, which is characterized by descriptions that seem appropriate to a sentimental novel. On April 10, the *New York Herald* reported: "Her face was pale and the features molded into lines of rare and exquisite beauty. Such eyes are rarely seen in a child—so large, so dark, and so wondering in their expression. In every lineament of the face could be read suffering, and its infantile freshness was marred by marks of fresh cuts and bruises; but as she smiled and with her tiny hands smoothed back from her forehead her wealth of brown hair one almost forgot these and the feeling of roused indignation burning within at thoughts of possible cruelty to one so young and fair and fragile."[27] The *New York Times* reporter went so far as to suggest that the child may have been a victim of some kind of class-tainted violence: "Taken together with the intelligent and rather refined appearance of the child, [the evidence offered] tends to the conclusion that she is the child of parents of some prominence in society, who, for some reason, have abandoned her to her present undeserved fate."[28] Her parents were not upper class but Irish immigrants, which hardly mattered at first to a press interested in stoking public interest.

Such embellishment diminished once the child's own description of her life was heard and reported. Here was a representative life, lived on the margins and a symbol both of individual sins of abuse and of a society's general acceptance of violence when practiced by the least of its members. Class-bound violence was for a moment brought into the sunlight, and the collective gasp that resulted drew attention to a system that not only did not prevent violence but also, because of its callousness and willful blindness, relegated the defenseless to the whims of their legal guardians. This child's life and rescue took on aspects of an epic battle against myriad evils and ultimately led to the creation of the New York Society of the Prevention of Cruelty to Children, in December 1874. In the hearing that decided her fate, Mary Ellen Wilson testified:

> My father and mother are both dead. I don't know how old I am. . . . I have never had but one pair of shoes, but I can't recollect when that was. I have no shoes or stockings this winter. . . . I have never had on a particle of flannel. My bed at night is only a piece of carpet, stretched on the floor underneath a window, and I sleep in my little undergarment, with a quilt over me. *I am never allowed to play with any children or have any company whatever. Mamma has been in the habit of whipping and beating me almost every day. She used to whip me with a twisted whip, a raw hide. The whip always left black and blue marks on my body. I have now on my head two black and blue marks, which were made by mamma with the whip, and a cut on the left side of my forehead, which was made by a pair of scissors in mamma's hand. She struck me with the scissors and cut me. I have no recollection of ever having been kissed, and have never been kissed by mamma. I have never been taken on mamma's lap, or caressed or petted.* I have never dared to speak to anybody, because if I did I would get whipped. . . . Whenever mamma went out I was locked up in the bedroom. . . . I have no recollection of ever being in the street in my life [emphasis added].[29]

Huckleberry Finn's mimicking of this statement is uncanny. What may have begun, for Clemens, with a memory of Hannibal's Finns and Blankenships and of a boy as a seemingly benign, if neglected and ostracized, village pariah becomes after 1874 something much more potent. The contrast between Huck as curiosity when he is introduced as a potential member of Tom's gang in *The Adventures of Tom Sawyer* and Huck as abused child as he describes his fear of Pap and the various marks of cow-hidings he wears in the opening chapters of *Adventures of Huckleberry Finn* is profound. As Clemens describes him during the chapters written in 1876, Huck Finn is, at least through fiction, a sibling to Mary Ellen Wilson. Mary's reported beatings with a cowhide (the whip was described in newspaper reports and played a prominent role in depositions and testimony) are seemingly replicated in Pap's attempt to reassert control over his son. In chapter 6, Huck reports: "But by and by pap got too handy with his hick'ry, and I couldn't stand it. I was all over welts. He got to going away so much, too, and locking me in. Once he locked me in and was gone three days. It was dreadful lonesome."[30] In chapter 5, Pap warns Huck, "I'll give you a cowhide" (24), and he threatens the boy. "He said he'd cowhide me till I was black and blue if I didn't raise money for him" (26). Clemens, in fact, changed his draft mention of a "rawhide" into the infamous "cowhide," which may be a bow to the image of the beaten and scared New York child. Mary's description, especially the mention of the whippings and her confinement for extended periods of time, may have been fodder for Clemens' version of Huck's story. It certainly seems to be an influence in the development of Huck's character in the final sections of *Tom Sawyer*. In Huck's tale, Clemens concentrates on Pap's callousness and violence. Huck, like small Mary Ellen Wilson, is isolated and beaten, and the primary actor in the violence aimed at his body and spirit is a parent.

Clemens was familiar with the violence that existed on the Hannibal frontier, and he ran its current beneath and through the nostalgia of his fiction. The story of Tom Sawyer is shaded with grave robbing, murder, and the directed threat of the racial and ethnic hybrid Joe; Huck's tale is much more severe in the explicit reach of Pap Finn and the various emotional and physical brutalities of the slave hunters, Grangerfords, Shepherdsons, Sherburn, the Duke, the King, and the mob that binds and shackles a free Jim. Clemens had seen the "trundle-bed trash" in the streets of New York in the 1850s, 1860s, and 1870s. Those prescient images, allied with the story of young Mary Ellen beaten and imprisoned in New York's tenements, would for a new parent have brought the issue of child welfare into sharp relief as a contemporary horror, perhaps especially for a father of daughters. In the end, Huck's tale is an extension of Mary's. It's a far distance from even the tarnished hymn of *The Adventures of Tom Sawyer*, and it is created within hearing of the voices of the Clemens girls: Susy and Clara and Jean are omnipresent in the Clemenses' life, and Clemens' fatherhood becomes the prism for his tales of children at risk from the violence of home and the disinterestedness of the community.

2

Horace Bushnell and Huck

Christian Nurture and *Adventures of Huckleberry Finn*

> The odor of the house will always be in his garments, and the internal difficulties with which he has to struggle will spring of the family seeds planted in his nature.
>
> —Horace Bushnell, *Christian Nurture*

By MIDCAREER (roughly 1876 though 1894), Samuel Clemens (influenced, I believe, by an abiding concern for his daughters and by the haunting memory of his dead son) devoted a major portion of his fiction to exploring the plight of children; he wrote social criticism with an eye toward reforming a world in conspiracy against the health and well-being of children. His preface to *The Adventures of Tom Sawyer* is instructive. He writes: "Although my book is intended mainly for the entertainment of boys and girls, I hope it will not be shunned by men and women on that account, for part of my plan has been to try to pleasantly remind adults of what they once were themselves, and of how they felt and thought and talked, and what queer enterprises they sometimes engaged in." What better way to establish adult interest in the plight of children than to describe a childhood embroidered with adult worry and adult prejudice?

Clemens' concern with children reflects the change in his own life precipitated by his marriage to Olivia in 1870. On June 25, 1870, Samuel Clemens sat down to pen a brief note to Charles Scribner and Company: "Dear Sirs, Please send me Dr Bushnell's volume entitled 'Christian Nurture,' to the above address, & charge to Yrs Truly, S. L. Clemens."[1] The Clemenses were in Elmira to help care for the dying Jervis Langdon, Livy's father. Livy was at the time pregnant with the Clemenses' first child. There is a sadness in realizing that the Clemenses began their preparations for parenthood simultaneously with the death of the Langdon patriarch. It's possible that they turned to Bushnell's volume while they looked to the future of their own family and searched for solace at the coming loss of Livy's father: Bushnell's liberal brand of congregationalism both influenced and was a reminder of the progressive ideals the Langdons had instilled in Livy; and the preacher's mentoring of Thomas K. Beecher and Joseph Twichell, both of whom officiated at the Clemenses' wedding, spoke to Clemens' spiritual interest and, more importantly, to his broadening social awareness. The book would have a mighty influence on Clemens, and while he and Livy would look to the ideas as a base for their parenting, for Clemens, Bushnell's small volume would furnish a good many insights that would affect both the overall character of the boy Huckleberry Finn and the social criticism that is at the heart of his tale.

In his chapter "What Christian Nurture Is" Bushnell sets out the focus for his spiritual and cultural concern. He writes: "We hold a piety of conquest rather than love. A kind of public piety that is strenuous and fiery on great occasions, but wants the beauty of holiness, wants constancy, singleness of aim, loveliness, purity, richness, blamelessness, and—if I may add another term not so immediately religious, but one that carries, by association, a thousand religious qualities—wants domesticity of character; wants them, I mean, not as compared with the perfect standard of Christ, but as compared with other examples of piety that have been given in former times, and others that are given now" (13). False piety is the enemy of domesticity and, as such, crushes the possibility of domestic virtue in its purest and most spiritual and redemptive form. For Bushnell, home was the focal point for spiritual instruction, and parents carried a heavy responsibility as models and arbiters of Christian values, values not contained within rituals or series of externally prompted acts; for Bushnell, "virtue still is rather a state of being than an act or series of acts" (30). And the home was the place that shaped that "state of being."

Bushnell's agenda is to instruct parents especially regarding their role in the spiritual health of children. It is, though, a lesson not restricted to parents, for the spiritual life of the home can be extended organically into the community. For

Bushnell, "All society is organic—the Church, the state, the school, the family . . . a pure, separate, individual man living *wholly* within, and from himself, is a mere fiction. No such person existed or ever can" (31). This idea of the social compact inhabits Clemens' heart and shapes his outlook on the relationship between and among individuals and their community. That interconnectedness will be a powerful lesson within Clemens' mature fiction: The ties that bind are weblike and anchor not only Clemens' characters to each other but also his readers to those characters and each other. Bushnell's focus on the Christian household has a direct influence on Clemens' exploration of domestic relations and especially of children forced by circumstance to make their way absent parents.

Bushnell's household is characterized by the intimate relations between parent and child: "If we narrowly examine the relation of parent and child, we shall not fail to discover something like a law of organic connection, as regards character, subsisting between them." This leads to a consideration of "whether a child is born in depravity, or whether the depraved character is superinduced afterwards" (27). The prevailing embrace of individualism by the mid-nineteenth-century American simplifies, perhaps oversimplifies, the idea that it is possible for the lone being (in this case the lone child) to create himself or herself. It is a denial of organic relations and fails to see "that character may be, to a great extent, only the free development of exercises previously wrought in us, or extended to us, when other wills had us within their sphere" (29). In effect, Bushnell questions a hyperindividualism or simplistic self-reliance that removes the individual from a social, and especially familial, context. The proper response to such a limiting view is Christian education that "begins with nurture and cultivation" (30).

Nurture and cultivation aim at encouraging the child to virtue and piety. The assumption is that villainy is neither natural nor spontaneous and neither is inclination or disinclination to piety. External ritual, rote lessons, and insisting that a child replicate outward or symbolic religiosity have no lasting effect on a child's spiritual development, nor does emphasizing the child's need to embrace conversion lead to redemption. For Bushnell,

> Simply to tell a child, as he just begins to make acquaintance with words, that he "must have a new heart before he can be good," is to inflict a double discouragement. . . . He is told that he must have a new heart *before* he can be good, not that he may hope to exercise a renewed spirit, in the endeavor to be good—why, then, attempt what must be worthless till something *previous* befalls him? Discouraged thus on every side, his tender

> soul turns hither and thither, in hopeless despair, and finally he consents to be what he must—a sinner against God, and that only. (50)

Children are, then, at genuine risk of a deep and relentless despair because they absorb the judgments of adults in home or community and are easy prey for facile and relentless definitions of sin. If this is true of children embraced by parents and family and community, how much truer will this be for those on the margins who either have no direct ties to a family or have been cut off (for whatever reason) or denied honest affection and care.

The question of conversion, the need for the individual child to admit a tendency to sin and to accept Christian faith is likewise worrisome. How can a child take steps to faith if he or she is continually held to an adult standard of contrition. Children are at a disadvantage when adults force upon them "notions of conversion that are mechanical and proper only to the adult age" (73). Such teaching ends in frustration and opens the child only to misunderstanding and, perhaps in extremes, to his or her becoming antireligious. In a long passage Bushnell lays out the peril:

> [Adults] indoctrinate [children] soundly in respect to their need of a new heart; tell them what conversion is, and how it comes to pass with grown people; pray that God will arrest them when they are old enough to be converted according to this manner; drill them, meantime, into all the constraints, separated from all the hopes and liberties of religion; turning all their little misdoings and bad tempers into evidence of their need of regeneration, and assuring them that all such signs must be upon them till after they have passed the change. Their nurture is a nurture of despair; and the bread of life itself, held before them as a fruit to be looked upon, but not tasted, till they are old enough to have it as grown people do, finally becomes repulsive, just because they have been so long repelled and fenced away from it. And so religion itself, pressed down upon them till they are fatally sored by its impossible claims, becomes their fixed aversion. (74)

Acting in bad faith, then, can grow at its most profound level to agnosticism (at best) and perhaps even to misanthropy.

Often, however, the parent (or adult acting in place of the parent) transfers his or her own spiritual despair to the child: "They propagate their own evil in the child, not by design, but under a law of moral infection" (100). That infection grows not by explicit teaching but instead by the models presented and the atmospheric connections. Organic relationships are, in the purest sense, hotbeds of moral and immoral lessons: "The spirit of the house is in the members by nurture; not by teaching, not by any attempt to communicate the same, but because it is in the air the children breathe" (101). In the end, moral disease is easily transmitted and, without some kind of intervention, the child will succumb to the tendency toward evil and break with the moral community: "The moral disease of the family he assuredly will take, and that, probably without even a question, or a cautious feeling started" and unless some person or institution intervenes "the organic spirit of the house will infallibly shape and subordinate his character" (107).

In a later chapter titled "Parental Qualifications," Bushnell builds his argument for the organic influence of parents and the dire results possible in a soured home. These parents demonstrate traits that call into question their fitness. Among these "vices" are sanctimony ("a saintly, or over-saintly air and manner, when there is a much inferior degree of sanctity in the life" [263]), bigotry, Christian fanaticism, censoriousness, disowning authority (especially God's authority), and anxiousness ("And nothing will so dreadfully torment the life of a child as to be perpetually teased by the anxious words, and looks, and interferences of this unhappy superintendence" [266]). Households that suffer such vices offer little or no spiritual or even physical protection to a child who must, instead, be constantly on guard for his own safety. The problem, of course, is that an atmosphere so poisoned will lead only to destruction, and the path to that destruction is cobbled with a variety of lies. Still later, Bushnell aims at the very idea that words and methods can by themselves take the place of an organic life and the models created within such a home. Truth does not depend on logic and language; truth separated from the very life lived cannot and does not enter the home: "No truth is really taught by words, or interpreted by intellectual and logical methods; truth must be lived into meaning, before it can be truly known" (370). From dissipation comes dissipation; from mercy comes mercy, redemption, and reconstruction. The questions of virtue and worth brought Clemens to Huckleberry Finn.

Prompted in part by ideas articulated by Bushnell, Clemens, beginning with his postmarriage writings in the mid-1870s, explores transplanting virtue in the young. His premier work is *Adventures of Huckleberry Finn*. When he finished *The Adventures of Tom Sawyer*, Sam Clemens wrote from Elmira to Howells: "By & by I shall take a boy of twelve & run him through life (in the first person) but not Tom Sawyer—he would not be a good character for it."[2] Roughly a year later and again from the Langdon summer home at Quarry Farm, he wrote to Howells, "I . . .

began another boy's book—more to be at work than anything else. I have written 400 pages on it—therefore, it is nearly half done. It is Huck Finn's Autobiography. I like it only tolerably well, as far as I have got, & may possibly pigeonhole or burn the MS when it is done."[3] By the end of that summer, Clemens had written himself into the conversation between Huck and Buck Grangerford (which appears in chapter 18 of the completed novel); he ends that conversation abruptly when Huck asks Buck, "What's a feud?" (146). Clemens returned to *Huckleberry Finn* in March 1880, then again in late 1882 and during the summer of 1883. He revises the manuscript and oversees the illustrations in 1884. In all, Samuel Clemens spent nearly eight years writing *Adventures of Huckleberry Finn*.

During this period, Samuel and Olivia Clemens are focused on their young family. Already the parents of two daughters, Susy and Clara, the Clemenses add Jean to their family in 1880. After the death of Langdon in 1872, the Clemenses hold even more tightly to their three girls. And it is entirely possible that Susy's privileged place in her parents' hearts is directly tied to a combination of grief and protectiveness that transfers their emotions to her after the death of her older brother. The girls become a primary influence on Clemens' writing, not as a direct allusion but certainly as a continual offstage presence that sparks Clemens' social sensibilities and drives his evolving sense of social justice. Having children drastically alters Clemens' outlook on the world and makes him more sensitive to broad issues and more interested in how his own writing can help focus readers' attentions, especially on issues that affect children and the communities in which they live.

A quick survey of Clemens' writing prior to fatherhood shows, I believe, that he shifts to a deeper and more biting social criticism once he realizes that his daughters will be forced to live in the world that he can help create. His early journalism, while at times displaying strong outrage at inequality, is dominated by a wild humor more tied to the long tradition of the tall tale and burlesque. Even his swipes at political parties and politicians seem tied more to a disgust at folly and greed than the larger issue of social compassion. When he approaches questions of moral instruction, Clemens turns to parody of the simplistic moral instruction of Sunday school books, such as in "The Christmas Fireside" (1865) and "The Story of the Good Little Boy Who Did Not Prosper" (1870), to the overblown flourishes of missionary zeal, such as in "The Story of Mamie Grant, the Child-Missionary" (1868), and to a combination of Sunday school morality and hatred for immigrants, such as in "Disgraceful Persecution of a Boy" (1870). An early dialogue-driven piece, "Colloquy Between a Slum Child and a Moral Mentor" (1868), hints of Clemens' later interest in the situation of the lost child; however, even here the situation and language aim at contrast and incongruity rather than a response to social conditions. The piece has more in common with the exchange between Scotty Briggs and the minister as they discuss Buck Fanshaw's funeral in *Roughing It* than with the later spiritual conflict between Miss Watson and Huck.

The combination of domestic and family concerns and fiction writing becomes a potent brew as Clemens begins to sharpen his voice as a critic of his contemporary American society and the growing social demands from and worries over the place of children within that society. Often, readers approach Clemens' "boy" books assuming that they are propelled by nostalgia and by a more or less affectionate recreation of an ideal childhood. The reality, of course, is that all of Clemens' writings grew out of his interest in contemporary issues. While he at times set the tales in various historical periods, the issues and concerns that sharpen the tales are part of Clemens' own times. Nowhere is that more clear than in his creation of Huckleberry Finn, a boy who finds himself very much alone, for all intents and purposes an orphan.

The genesis of *Huckleberry Finn* is complicated. While most approaches to the novel emphasize Clemens' nostalgia and childhood experience as the germ for the character and the tale, the whole of the novel may have been influenced more by Clemens' contemporary concerns over family and the worries of child rearing. Despite readings and interpretations of the novel that argue for Clemens' exclusive focus on race, placing the novel within a larger context of American realism brings it in line with mid-nineteenth-century worries over the status of the disenfranchised (both white and black) and of children turned out into the streets as the result of immigration and economic stress. What seems a historical novel on the experiences of an antebellum child is, in actuality, a book about a boy who chooses exile from a broken domestic life and a community that ignores his pain, insisting instead on the sanctity of parental rights, even when the exercise of those rights raises welts on a child's back. *Adventures of Huckleberry Finn* cannot be so easily characterized as nostalgia or idyll. It is a book about the failure of a father to properly nurture his son and about the failure of a community to understand the depths of that father's and that son's ruin. If Clemens thought that *Tom Sawyer* was a hymn, he offers *Huckleberry Finn* as a dirge, a lament for the socially and spiritually dead.

After Clemens discovered the power in the image of Huck at the end of *The Adventures of Tom Sawyer*, he began to plan for Huck's return as the narrator of his own tale. Interestingly, at the same time that he is creating Huck's voice, Clemens is also carefully studying and recording comments and stories that grow out of the day-to-day experiences with his daughters, which he collects in "The Small Foolishnesses of Susy and Bay Clemens (Infants)." Clemens worked on that experience off and on from 1874 (when Susy would have been two) through 1884 and used it as a repository for a broad collection of comments on the language, thinking processes, and perspectives on events that highlight his daughters' understanding of the world around them.

Of course, the adolescent Huck is much beyond the childlike language that Clemens recorded in his manuscript; however, there is clearly a link between the girls and the world that Huck inhabits, even if that link is built out of contrast. For example, clearly the Clemens daughters experience a level of social and economic privilege that Huck can never attain. Clemens understood the privilege that his daughters enjoyed and the safety in which they lived, and he appreciated that safety and comfort as a cocoon few children would know: He knew the dangers facing children both from his own experience of deprivation and from his observations of children who were at risk both in frontier and urban settings. All of that informs the backstory Clemens creates for Huck.

The basic design of Huck may have come from Clemens' childhood and Hannibal's Tom Blankenship; however, the full character is shaped and shaded by a swirl of contemporary concerns, from child abuse to alcoholism, from the tide of immigration to the dire urban poverty and slum tenements. Huck's story, though poignant, is unremarkable for many nineteenth-century children. Huck's mother is dead and only a shadow memory. She is, perhaps, the catalyst for the boy's drive to find some place of comfort and peace in a community that seems at times hostile and often indifferent to him. His father, both a violent drunk and an opportunist, returns only after he hears about Huck's fortune and sees a chance to claim a prize. He is abusive, especially when he faces the possibility that his son will have opportunities that were never his own (think of the home atmosphere and patriarchal violence of Stephen Crane's *Maggie: A Girl of the Streets*, published only eight years after *Huckleberry Finn*; Twain is working both in a similar frame and with a similar image of broken homelife, though he transports the urban life to the antebellum frontier). The absence of genuine and Christian compassion is most clear.

Pap comes back to town not only for the wealth that he has heard is Huck's but, and perhaps more importantly, to inoculate the boy from any form of economic or intellectual or spiritual achievement. Even basic literacy skills intimidate and infuriate Pap:

> You've put on considerable many frills since I been away. I'll take you down a peg before I get done with you. You're educated too, they say; can read and write. You think you're better'n your father, now, don't you, because he can't? *I*'ll take that out of you. Who told you you might meddle

> with such hifalut'n foolishness, hey? . . . And looky-here—you drop that school, you hear? I'll learn people to bring up a boy to put on airs over his own father and let on to be better'n what *he* is. You lemme catch you fooling around that school again, you hear? Your mother couldn't read, and she couldn't write, nuther, before she died. None of the family couldn't, before *they* died. *I* can't; and here you're swelling yourself up like this. I ain't the man to stand it—you hear? . . . Now looky-here, you stop that putting on frills. I won't have it. I'll lay for you, my smarty; and if I catch you about that school I'll tan you good. First you know you'll get religion, too. I never seen such a son. (24)

Pap's phobia about reading and writing runs in tandem with his hatred of government and of the social acceptance of blacks. His anger is aimed at what literacy represents: better living conditions and a stronger place within society than any he has had or will have. His reference to his dead wife and to Huck's dead mother is especially unnerving because, by extension, it accuses Huck of disloyalty toward his mother and of leaving behind his family for the sheltering embrace of the Widow. That would hit Huck particularly hard, given his continual search for security but his constant ambivalence toward accepting the Widow's hospitality and compassion. Pap conjures memories of the dead (which, with the reference to other family members who supposedly died illiterate, can also mean dead brothers or sisters) to scare Huck back under his control. His mention of religion is also poignant: Pap's hatred of religion pushes Huck further into a spiritual darkness and sets a clear expectation that no one should influence a child's faith in place of his family, or in this case his father. It is, in short, paternalism run wild.

With the name Finn, Clemens seems to be looking to the experience of the socially ostracized Irish, and while there is reason to think that Pap's figure is shaded with assumptions based on stereotypes, there is no reason to think that Clemens was purposely playing up those stereotypes to cast a broad charge at an ethnic group. Instead, it's possible to see Pap's behavior as a logical, and perhaps expected, result of a social policy that both disenfranchises him and establishes a clear and solid set of constraints that work against any kind of economic and social progress. Pap is bitter because of the destruction of his own life's chances and has given himself over to white trash reasoning, which aims his more vehement bile at the only group that has even less power than his own: slaves.

Pap, then, while he plays a relatively minor role in the novel, is a prime influence on Huck and on Huck's ways of thinking about and living in the world. Even after escaping Pap after a night of murderous rampage, Huck returns to the lessons that Pap taught, lessons about stealing to survive and, most importantly, about how to get along with adults who are hell-bent on violence and abuse. The main lesson Pap teaches Huck is that when faced with superior strength and absolute blind self-interest, it's always better to disappear, to not call attention to yourself. Huck voices that first commandment of the abused when he says first of Miss Watson, who is a practitioner of her own form of fundamentalist abuse by insisting that Huck aim for heaven: "Well, I couldn't see no advantage in going where she was going, so I made up my mind I wouldn't try for it. But I never said so, because it would only make trouble, and wouldn't do no good" (4). Later, when confronting the Duke and the King, Huck says: "It didn't take me long to make up my mind that these liars warn't no kings or dukes, at all, but just low-down humbugs and frauds. But I never said nothing, never let on; kept it to myself; it's the best way, then you don't have no quarrels, and don't get into trouble. If they wanted us to call them kings and dukes, I hadn't no objections, long as it would keep peace in the family; and it warn't no use to tell Jim, so I didn't tell him. *If I never learned nothing else out of pap, I learnt that the best way to get along with his kind of people is to let them have their own way*" (165, emphasis added). Silence is the key.

Such overwhelming silence shuts off the possibilities either of conventional religion or of social behavior marked with a sense of ethics and justice. Clemens presents Pap's head-in-the-sand approach to child nurture as a repudiation of robust social Christianity and a direct refusal of the ideals of any spiritual (and even social) compact. Pap is interested only in the physical world and only in his own place and comfort in that world. It is a lesson that Huck internalizes, and it is a point of view toward the world that keeps Huck in a constant state of apprehension and primes his hyperactive skepticism when considering the motives and conduct of adults.

From the beginning of Huck's tale, he has struggled with the reality of his outsider status within the community. In contemporary interpretations of Mark Twain's *Adventures of Huckleberry Finn* critics continue to emphasize the variations of freedom experienced by Huck and Jim during their experiences on raft and on land. We are still captive to Leo Marx's argument in "Mr. Eliot, Mr. Trilling, and *Huckleberry Finn*" (1956):

> That theme [which forms the skeleton of the novel] is highlighted by the juxtaposition of sharp images of contrasting social orders: the micro-cosmic community Huck and Jim establish aboard the raft and the actual

> society which exists along the Mississippi's banks. The two are separated by the river, the road to freedom upon which Huck and Jim must travel. Huck tells us what the river means to them when, after the Wilks episode, he and Jim must once again shove their raft into the current: "It *did* seem so good to be free again and all by ourselves on the big river, and nobody to bother us." The river is indifferent. But its sphere is relatively uncontaminated by the civilization they flee, and so the river allows Huck and Jim some measure of freedom at once, the moment they set foot on Jackson's Island or the raft. Only on the island and the raft do they have a chance to practice the idea of brotherhood to which they are devoted. "Other places do seem so cramped and smothery," Huck explains, "but a raft don't. You feel free and easy and comfortable on a raft." The main thing is freedom.[4]

In 1953 Marx gave voice to an idea that solidified Huck as a new hero for the American century and the raft as a utopian, egalitarian icon—John Winthrop's "City upon a Hill" as floating refuge and model of brotherhood, though a brotherhood that is theoretical rather than actual, taken out of any racial and class-bound, and therefore real, context. This contrast of raft and shore communities canonized a particular reading and effectively suspended our search for meaning. Identifying this contrast became an end unto itself; it became *the* end and not a means to understand the dynamic of being in the world. Critics still find that a comfort, a lesson peculiarly shaped by the metaphor of the journey but that fails to acknowledge the passing world. And a lesson that, perhaps more, fails to understand Clemens' debt to spirituality and faith in the most foundational teachings of Christianity. We need to widen our view.

For many readers and scholars, Clemens' interest in setting up an alternative society of two is sparked by a none-too-subtle rage against oppression. In reality, of course, while Huck and Jim are physically isolated from larger communities, they must remain closely tied to community values and mores because they have been brought up within and therefore will most definitely conform to the general teachings and ideology of their society. Clemens' rage against the bias expressed within the dominant ideology is somehow seen as enough to break his characters from the laws and especially the customs that have shaped them intellectually and spiritually: Clemens' criticism of the dominant ideology prompts his characters to transcend the limits of their time and place and context. Ironically, given the emphasis on the metaphysical, there has been a reluctance to admit that the freedom the characters gain or work toward is restricted, and there is a companion reluctance to ascribe to Clemens any kind of religious or spiritual belief or motive; as a result, Clemens is grounded almost entirely within a secular, agnostic, and at times atheistic tradition. Clemens' humanism, we are told, informs his notions of man's, here Huck's, innate goodness.

All of that is presented as driving Clemens' explicit interest in and commitment to *racial* justice. In *Adventures of Huckleberry Finn* freedom, it is argued, is jeopardized once the civilized world encroaches on the raft with the arrival of the Duke and the King, an interpretation that is itself simplistic: The stresses of the world are *never* displaced from the raft because of the unambiguous racial and class markers that identify Huck and Jim. Such critical myopia seems to me to rely on both our own twenty-first-century understanding of race (with a still too rarely examined component of class awareness) and our creating in Clemens both an unreasonable and unrealistic capacity for tolerance. We have created the image of Sam Clemens as social sage and antiracist savior and have been deliberate about and very successful at installing that image as a part of our cultural iconography. Sanctifying (sanitizing?) Clemens makes us feel better about ourselves and about our work as literary critics: Emphasizing his potential to transcend race reinforces our own superiority. At the same time, we argue that Clemens held no spiritual foundation that would inform his critique, and we state more or less confidently that Clemens' embrace of charity is devoid of a religious or spiritual spine. To challenge the notion that race is at the heart of Clemens' social agenda is today heretical and leads to charges of apostasy. The issue, however, is not whether Sam Clemens worked for racial justice. At times he did. At times he didn't (most notably in his lifelong and unmovable prejudice toward Native Americans). The issue is why we examine Clemens so exclusively through the prism of race, most often restricted to the duality of black/white relations. Racial awareness was not Clemens' muse; nor was it Clemens' primary topic.

One of Clemens', and therefore Huck's, anxieties *is* related to race. It is a trial for Huck as he literally writes his way through to some kind of relationship with Jim. Rather than reach a clear and definite and easy tie to Jim, Huck remains almost steadfastly ambivalent toward Jim, whose presence reminds Huck of his own marginal status and lack of ties to any community. Their relationship (most often touted as the primary lesson in the novel) is and remains essentially unresolved at the end of the tale, complicated by the unambiguous status of a manumitted slave in the Deep South whose one desire is to be reunited with his family, on the one hand, and Huck's announced plan to "light out for the territory ahead of the rest," on the other (362). Huck seems to have had enough of race conflict (of conflict of any kind), or at least enough of the psychic pain caused by his own moral ambivalence. He seems to relish the thought of disappearing into the landscape before he can become involved in Jim's seemingly inevitable and quite possibly doomed attempt to rescue his family. Leaving ahead of the rest will allow Huck to avoid true abolitionist work; disavowing Jim's claim to his family keeps Huck far from a moral battle that holds little real interest and, within the context of the novel, no possible hope for success. While Jim holds to the dream, to Huck such an errand courts one more physical and psychic beating. Racism, however, is one form of prejudice, one set of chains. I think that neither Jim nor Huck is capable of a triumph over such a cultural force. For Huck there is another profoundly personal challenge.

There is a darkness manifest in Huck's loneliness and isolation as he struggles with and chafes against chains of domestic abuse and alcoholism and desperate and soul-sick loneliness. Huck gives voice to his loneliness early in chapter 1:

> Miss Watson she kept pecking at me, and it got tiresome and lonesome. . . . I went up to my room with a piece of candle and put it on the table. Then I set down in a chair by the window and tried to think of something cheerful, but it warn't no use. I felt so lonesome I most wished I was dead. The stars was shining, and the leaves rustled in the woods ever so mournful; and I heard an owl, away off, who-whooing about somebody that was dead, and a whippowill and a dog crying about somebody that was going to die; and the wind was trying to whisper something to me and I couldn't make out what it was, and so it made the cold shivers run over me. Then away out in the woods I heard that kind of sound a ghost makes when it wants to tell about something that's on its mind and can't make itself understood, and so can't rest easy in its grave and has to go about that way every night grieving. I got so down-hearted and scared, I did wish I had some company. Pretty soon a spider went crawling up my shoulder, and I flipped it off and it lit in the candle; and before I could budge it was all shriveled up. I didn't need anybody to tell me that was an awful bad sign and would fetch me some bad luck, so I was scared and most shook the clothes off me. I got up and turned around in my tracks three times and crossed my breast every time; and then I tied up a little lock of my hair with a thread to keep the witches away. But I hadn't no confidence. You do that when you've lost a horse-shoe that you've found, instead of nailing it up over the door, but I hadn't ever heard anybody say it was any way to keep off bad luck when you'd killed a spider. (4–5)

Clearly, Clemens is attuned to the cadence of loneliness and the desperation of the dispossessed. Throwaway children were plentiful in the nineteenth century. They are just as (more?) plentiful in the twenty-first. So are throwaway adults. Truth be told, many read this opening monologue and hear a friend's or a family member's voice. Sometimes we hear our own. And it scares the hell out of us. Huck's life is not so distant as we might like, need, or want to believe: We look to the students sitting in front of us and find Huck's cousins still very much alive in our world.

Adventures of Huckleberry Finn is shaped by Huck's worry over his inability to find emotional comfort and, recognized only by some readers, his anger at a community whose customs keep him at arm's length and whose laws deliver him over to his raging and abusive father. Huck's longing to belong somewhere, to have the stability of a home, is palpable as he writes his story. We certainly feel his anxiety as we read; however, few readers are able to acknowledge the deep and abiding anger that colors Huck's approach to the world and to those with whom he comes into contact. While Clemens seems to soften that anger as Huck finds small bits of peace on the river, there is no doubt that the young boy has too often been the butt of a community's prejudice and too often been on the receiving end of paternal death threats to be at ease or forgiving of an adult world seemingly bent on administering physical pain or spiritual suffocation. Pap is a genuine threat, so much so that Huck withholds from the reader the evidence of his father's death, admitting it only at the end of his narrative (recall, Huck is writing the story as he waits for Tom Sawyer to heal from the bullet wound; as any autobiographer, he knows the full end of the story even when he begins the telling). And even the combined maternal compassion of the Widow Douglas or Aunt Sally cannot rid Huck of a resentment and anger sparked by the memory of a now long-dead mother (an anger and disappointment so deep that he never even mentions her name). In fact, none of the women Huck finds can replace his dead mother, try as they might (the Widow and Aunt Sally) or as he might wish them to (Rachel Grangerford or even Mary Jane Wilkes). Huck seems hell-bent on holding on to her memory, as he hears the voices of her ghost and (perhaps) only longs to be joined to her again.

Huck's anxiety prompts questions regarding the nature of family and a community's responsibility to the poor in its midst and the need to recognize and address social and domestic abuse. Like Walt Whitman, Clemens offers an iconoclastic belief that marginal voices must be heard. Huck is close kin to Whitman's "long dumb voices." More to the point, Samuel Clemens' characterization of Huck as a good-hearted child struggling with a deformed conscience has been, I think, wrongly read to suggest that Huck is an innocent or at least a benign presence. He is not. He is a genuine and disturbing threat to the society Clemens' readers inhabit. After all, despite Clemens' insistence that he wrote for the masses, his readers were most often middle or upper class. To them Huck is an untouchable. He is most dangerous not only because of his feral existence but also because he reminds readers of their complicity in a society that disposes of people—of children especially—in service to financial stability, material comfort, and spiritual laziness.

Clemens' image of Huck seems in fact a good deal more suggestive of the waste and debris of mid-nineteenth-century tenement life than of any recollection of the frontier. The catastrophic plight of the urban poor may be more vivid for Clemens' readers who faced the dilemma of Christian charity. Huck's story echoes the warning of the Beatitudes. Perhaps more rightly, it is Clemens' equivalent of Kurt Vonnegut's *Slaughterhouse-Five* interpretation of Kilgor Trout's lesson of the crucifixion: "Before you kill somebody, make absolutely sure he isn't well connected. . . . 'There are right people to lynch.' Who? People not well connected. So it goes."[5] Jim is not well connected. We see that. But Huck too is not well connected. And we have been slow to see that and reluctant to think it important.

Tom Sawyer saw it right away, which is why he bullies Huck so energetically and effectively. In the end, Huck's skepticism runs much deeper than a mistrust of Tom Sawyer's childish games that informs the novel's opening chapters; his reluctance to challenge Tom Sawyer during the evasion episode grows out of the "lesson" of silence. When Tom enthusiastically joins Huck in his quest to "steal" Jim out of slavery, he has become, for Huck, one more example of the duplicity of the adult world: "Well, I let go all holts, then, like I was shot. It was the most astonishing speech I ever heard—and I'm bound to say Tom Sawyer fell, considerable, in my estimation. Only I couldn't believe it. Tom Sawyer a *nigger stealer!*" (284). Since the end of *Tom Sawyer,* Tom has left behind the toys and pastimes of the child and has accepted his place as the enforcer of the community values. Huck is struck dumb, and in order to get along, he says nothing "because it would only make trouble, and wouldn't do no good." In his most extreme commitment, Tom has joined Pap's solipsistic community and Huck has already "learnt that the best way to get along with [Pap's] kind of people is to let them have their own way." Miss Watson, Tom Sawyer, the Duke, the King: All are Pap's kind of people.

Clemens forces us to ask, whether we, like Tom Sawyer, use others' poverty to *our* best advantage? Have we, like Tom and all of St. Petersburg and its ilk, backed away from the Seven Spiritual Works of Mercy: teach the ignorant, counsel the doubtful, console the sad, reprove the sinner, forgive the offender, bear with the oppressive and troublesome, pray. Have we set aside the Seven Corporal Works of Mercy: feed the hungry, give drink to the thirsty, clothe the naked, shelter the homeless, visit the sick and prisoners, ransom captives, bury the dead. Mercy, spiritual or corporal, should not demand payment. It should not rub out individual dignity. Clemens understood moral myopia, and he wrote to contest the comfort and selfishness that grows out of narcissistic self-righteousness. *Adventures of Huckleberry Finn*, then, is harsh. It is meant to be. The reality of slavery contributes to that harshness, but it is a symptom of a larger contagion: the dominance of ecclesiastic and civil law over mercy.

Clemens, like Aeschylus in *Prometheus Bound*, conjures the two vigorous henchmen of Zeus—Might and Violence. They revel in human frailty: they drink with Pap Finn; they terrify Huck to the point he accepts patricide as a way out; they stoke the hate of the Grangerfords and Shepherdsons that ends with the trauma of Buck Grangerford's death; they incite the murder of Boggs and encourage the mob that faces Sherburn; they whet the greed and lechery of the Duke and the King; and they invigorate the posse that chains and returns Jim to the Phelps farm. We stand watch with Huck as Might and Violence consort with the seven deadly sins: Pride, Covetousness, Envy, Wrath, Gluttony, Sloth, Lechery. They sew alienation and exploitation. They feast on meager pickings. Their fight is so vicious because the stakes are so small. And Jim and Huck escape with their lives only momentarily since the novel offers no real relief from a general anxiety. There are too many threats crouching silently off stage awaiting their cue.

Adventures of Huckleberry Finn is about human menace and how the combined threat of might and violence drives two isolated and marginalized human beings into a fragile mutual protection pact. When Jim shows up on Jackson's island, Huck is thrilled to have company; Jim is overjoyed to find Huck alive—Huck will give him both protection from a charge of murder (Jim is thought to have killed Huck) and the cover of whiteness for his escape. Each needs the other. But it is the desperate bond of the powerless and indigent; the white boy seared by poverty and abuse and the black man forced into deadly flight clearly cannot consider independence. Neither boy nor man is able to conceptualize freedom. Jim's idea of freedom depends upon a vague sense of geography, the value of forty dollars, and an unrealistic dream of being reunited with his family; Huck's definition is always freedom *from* never freedom *to*. Both can conceptualize a temporary rest from pain, a fleeting moment of comfort. After Buck Grangerford's murder, Huck reflects: "I was powerful glad to get away from the feuds, and so was Jim to get away from the swamp. We said there warn't no home like a raft, after all. Other places do seem so cramped up and smothery, but a raft don't. You feel mighty free and easy and comfortable on a raft" (155). Only for a short time, and in the company of memories that haunt so completely and irrevocably that they cannot be articulated, Huck, retelling Buck's death scene, admits, "I ain't agoing to tell all that happened—it would make me sick again if I was to do that. I wished I hadn't ever come ashore that night, to see such things. I ain't ever going to shut of them—lots of times I dream about them" (123). Huck is struck dumb by the vision of the dead boy, and Buck becomes, like Huck's mother, one more loss that will be suffered in a silence that reinforces anger and resentment. Rather than the great elegy for American individualism and unchained movement, Huck's story emphasizes the destructive effects of corporate thought and of a system that pits the least powerful (Pap Finn as white trash; the slave community) against each other to protect those who profit from inequality.

It also, and perhaps more cogently, presents the tale of a child brought up separated from any notion of genuine religious or spiritual value. Throughout the story, Huck struggles with the question of prayer. Most often, he uses prayer as an avenue for deal making with God: If I pray, then I will get this thing I want. And he wants a series of things, from gingerbread to a real and lasting family. But as Emerson warns in "Self-Reliance," "Prayer that craves a particular commodity,—anything less than all good,—is vicious. . . . [P]rayer as a means to effect a private end, is theft and meanness. It supposes dualism and not unity in nature and consciousness. As soon as the man is at one with God, he will not beg. He will see that all prayer is action." Huck is fully encased in false prayer and has no deep understanding of genuine piety. He is lost because he has never been taught the value of prayer and the strength to self-worth that is possible in righteous action. Huck is emblematic of Bushnell's wild child who has no filial teacher, no model of true faith. He has had the Widow Douglas and Miss Watson, and he has had Pap.

That is why Huck's attempt to write his conscience clean by informing Miss Watson of Jim's incarceration ends with his "sin." As Huck works through the problem of reporting Jim, he runs through a series of rationalizations. In a telling moment, Huck suggests that even slavery is acceptable if you are close to those you care about and who care about you: "Once I said to myself it would be a thousand times better for Jim to be a slave at home where his family was, so long as he'd got to be a slave, and so I'd better write to Tom Sawyer and tell him to tell Miss Watson where he was" (268). Huck is sufficiently astute to realize that Tom would be an excellent conduit for such news: Tom is in Huck's mind a representative of the social system. Huck concludes, however, that not only would Jim suffer for his running away but also Huck would be blamed to abetting the escape: "It would get around that Huck Finn helped a nigger get his freedom; and if I was to ever see anybody from that town again, I'd be ready to get down and lick his boots for shame" (268). And here all Miss Watson's spiritual guidance and Pap's depravity take their toll. Huck sees himself as damned, even though he has no concept of what that means:

> The more I studied about this, the more my conscience went to grinding me, and the more wicked, and low-down and ornery I got to feeling. And at last, when it hit me all of a sudden that here was the plain hand of Providence slapping me in the face and letting me know my wickedness was being watched all the time from up there in heaven, whilst I was stealing a poor old woman's nigger that hadn't ever done me no harm, and now was showing me there's One that's always on the lookout, and ain't agoing to allow no such miserable doings to go only just so fur and no further, I most dropped in my tracks I was so scared. Well, I tried the best I could to kinder soften it up somehow for myself, by saying I was brung up wicked, and so I warn't so much to blame; but something inside of me kept saying, "There was the Sunday School, you could a gone to it; and if you'd a done it they'd a learnt you, there, that people that acts as I'd been acting about that nigger goes to everlasting fire. (268–69)

The reality of Huck's existential crisis drives him to see himself as polluted and without grace, incapable, in fact, of obtaining grace. Here is the majesty of Clemens' point: Huck's realization that you "can't pray a lie" is linked to the fact that he was never fully taught to pray at all. The prayers that were said over him by Miss Watson and the rants and curses that were fed to him while with Pap conspire to eliminate any genuine and righteous action. He acts, but he acts out of desperation and with an assumption of his gracelessness. In chapter 16, just after a close call with a set of slave hunters (which ends up enriching Huck and Jim by forty dollars), Huck calculates his responsibility for aiding an escaped slave:

> I knowed very well I had done wrong, and I see it warn't no use for me to try to learn to do right; a body that don't get *started* right when he's little, ain't got no show—when the pinch comes there ain't nothing to back him up and keep him to his work, and so he gets beat. Then I thought a minute, and says to myself, hold on—spose you'd a done right and give Jim up; would you felt better than what you do now? No, says I, I'd feel

> bad—I'd feel just the same way I do now. Well, then, says I, what's the use of you learning to do right, when it's troublesome to do right and ain't no trouble to do wrong, and the wages is just the same? I was stuck. I couldn't answer that. So I reckoned I wouldn't bother now more about it, but after this always do whichever come handiest at the time. (127)

Huck's reflection does not lead to a moral choice; rather, he is caught up in a swirl of self-interest and leans toward action that leads to emotional comfort. Besides, he sees himself as damned, and, to be honest, he is. He has not been given a foundation in moral thought, nor has he been schooled by individuals able to serve as moral teachers or examples. Even Huck's notion of prayer is warped. Besides his experiment with prayer to request material goods (which cheapens and negates the worth of the prayer), he also understands that prayer is linked to the class of person who is praying. When the bread that is set adrift in hopes it will settle over his corpse in the days after his escape from Pap makes its way to him on the shore of Jackson's Island, Huck observes: "I says, now I reckon the widow or the parson or somebody prayed that this bread would find me, and here it has gone and done it. So there ain't no doubt but there is something in that thing. That is, there's something in it when a body like the widow or the parson prays, but it don't work for me, and I reckon it don't work for only just the right kind" (47). Huck is without faith and without hope.

Bushnell's teaching drives Clemens' theology here. To repeat the epigram at the beginning of this chapter: "The odour of the house will always be in his garments, and the internal difficulties with which he has to struggle will spring of the family seeds planted in his nature." Huck is a child of the Finn household; he is incapable of doing right because he has never been schooled in right. His action is self-serving. He might not be able to pray a lie, but he is, in the end, able to convince himself that a lie can spark action. It is the reader, however, that places the moral gloss on Huck's action. The reality is that Huck is no reformer, and he is no Christian. He has no reference point for such reform or belief.

Adventures of Huckleberry Finn is not a moral guidebook. It is a mirror. It is a puzzle. Clemens challenges us to confront lives spent one step from oblivion and our own complicity in injustice. It is time now to consider whether we have traded our love for the real and engagement in genuine political action for a blind hope in racial understanding by way of time spent with Huck and Jim on a raft. Huck's proclamation "All right, then, I'll go to hell" (271) is no epiphany. It is a recapitulation of a decision he made months earlier in the Widow Douglas' parlor when he is badgered by Miss Watson about the value of her heaven: "Then she told me all about the bad place, and I said I wished I was there. She got mad, then, but I didn't mean no harm. All I wanted was to go somewheres; all I wanted was a change. I wasn't particular. She said it was wicked to say what I said; said she wouldn't say it for the whole world; *she* was going to live so as to go to the good place. Well, I couldn't see no advantage in going where she was going, so I made up my mind I wouldn't try for it. But I never said so, because it would only make trouble, and wouldn't do no good" (3–4). Huck's decision to remain silent is not stoic. He is defeated. More's the pity, we, like Huck, resort to silence as the only safe response to the world.

All of that suggests that there is more to Clemens' story than an exclusive interest in race-driven social issues. There is local concern. There is family hope and family pain. Personal experience, a life of loss, uncertainty, and anxiety both over the health and well-being of his own children and an ability to see in their lives both promise and potential for loss pushed Clemens to write fiction that demanded that readers consider the plight of his child characters and, therefore, the plight of children facing down an antagonistic world. As a father, Clemens could not help but wonder what the world would offer his daughters. As a writer, Clemens could not help but write stories with "a pen warmed in hell." Clemens' social critique was energized with the hope that telling a story could influence readers to act for good and moral purpose. And it is Huck's shredded hope that is never far from the surface of Clemens' conscience—and perhaps our own.

3

Children of the Urban Poor

Tom Canty and Edward VI

Day before yesterday I encountered Mrs. Harriet Beecher Stowe on the sidewalk. She took both my hands and said with strong fervency that surprised the moisture into my eyes—"I am reading your Prince and the Pauper for the fourth time, and I *know* it is the best book for young folks ever written."
—*Mark Twain's Notebooks and Journals*, April 12, 1887 entry

CLEMENS ENDED HIS first concentrated stint of work on *Adventures of Huckleberry Finn* at the moment that Huck sits with his *Doppelgänger* Buck Grangerford and asks, "What's a feud?" Huck, though he has been in the middle of constant battles throughout the opening chapters of his story (the battle between the Widow Douglas and Pap Finn, the battle between Judge Thatcher and Pap, the battle between Miss Watson and Widow Douglas, the battle between the general St. Petersburg community and the willful Pap), is unable to fathom that a family as intact and as comfortable as the Grangerfords could enter into a devil's pact to kill another extended and similarly ensconced family. Huck is unable to recognize the motives for the feud and is caught midway between opposing forces determined to kill or be killed. Clemens here found himself in a dilemma much more challenging than whether Huck and Jim would wash up on shore after the destruction of the raft (a natural break in the tale of runaways, this episode was for years thought to be the most logical place for Clemens to stop writing the first large installment). Clemens could go no further without reviewing the first half of the novel so that he could better understand the motivations and implications and the dire results of a feud between comparably closed-minded families.

Unable to completely put aside the issues generated in *Huckleberry Finn*, Clemens recapitulates Huck's tale in the guise of Tom Canty's and Edward VI's escapades in *The Prince and the Pauper* (1881). By the time he began to tackle the tale of the young pauper and the soon-to-be king, it is likely that Clemens was steeped in the issues of at-risk children and the challenge to a society (or a city) with few resources (and even less moral will) to address the problem. That knowledge had a hand in Huckleberry Finn's backstory, a story that while set in rural Missouri has a distinctly urban sensibility when laying out the plight of the throwaway child. When shifting to the story of the inverted twins, Clemens was prepared to mark the squalor of urban slums by creating the neighborhood of Offal Court, and he moved the story's setting from the banks of the Mississippi to sixteenth-century London, a move that was made by way of 1853 and 1870s New York. As a young itinerant printer, Clemens made his first extended journey east from Hannibal to New York hoping to find work and experience. What he found, of course, was a city whose streets teemed with a human tide, a vast percentage of whom were recently arrived and scrounging in the streets until they could find safe and comfortable quarters and the means to find a decent meal. Young Sam had never experienced the crush and pace of so great a city, and while he was acquainted with the face of rural poverty from his time on the borders of the Mississippi, he was unprepared for the reality of urban life, the throng of humanity, and the situation of the poor. His early letters offer a look at his wide-eyed and prejudiced view of the city:

> Of all the commodities, manufacturers—or whatever you please to call it—in New York, trundle-bed trash—children I mean—take the lead. Why from Cliff street, up to Frankfort to Nassau street, six of seven squares—my road to dinner—I think I could count two hundred brats. Niggers, mulattoes, quadroons, Chinese, and some the Lord no doubt originally intended to be white, but the dirt on whose faces leaves one uncertain to that fact, block up the little, narrow street; and to wade through this mass of human vermin, would raise the ire of the most patient person that ever lived. In going to and

> from my meals, I go by the way of Broadway—and to *cross* Broadway is the rub—but once across, it is *the* rub for two or three squares. My plan—and how could I choose another, when there *is* no other—is to get into the crowd; and when I get in, I am borne, and rubbed, and crowded along, and need scarcely trouble myself about using my own legs; and when I get out, it seems like I had been pulled to pieces and very badly put together again.[1]

Urban experience is a great deal noisier, dirtier, and more dangerous because of the host of unanticipated and uncontrolled litter of humanity. While over the next two decades Clemens would see an increasing share of urban squalor, whether in San Francisco or New York, or the streets of European and Middle Eastern cities, this virgin experience was telling and would sit beneath Clemens' memories, especially placed within the context of the shift in setting from *Tom Sawyer* and *Huckleberry Finn* to *The Prince and the Pauper*. By the late 1870s, Clemens was becoming more aware of the great stress of immigration and the urban poor. Having so much himself, both out of hard work and a good marriage, Clemens infuses his writing with class worries and class determinations.

That awareness can be seen in the opening pages of Clemens' English novel: Tom Canty is none other than Huck Finn transported back in time to face first the ire of his drunken and abusive father (and in a complete turn of the domestic assumption, a similarly abusive grandmother) and then the confusion of finding himself a resident of a comfortable home (palace) and unable to fathom the intrigues and stresses of family (and in court a kind of extended family) politics. Colonel Grangerford's authority has morphed into the aging and sickly Henry VIII; Jim's aid and watchful presence shifts to the careful and disenfranchised Miles Hendon. There is, then, a symbiotic connection between the two novels, a deep tie that Clemens recognized in his original plan to offer the two novels together as a package subscription. More than a pure marketing strategy, the pairing of the novels hints at their shared theme of children forced to make their own way in the world, a way that was most often blocked by greedy and abusive adults or a system known for its class privilege rather than its social justice.

However similar the journeys of Huck and Tom Canty and Edward, the settings for the tales are diametrically opposed: The Mississippi Valley, with its small towns and quintessential rural flavor, is very different from London's Offal Court, with its slum housing and chaotic city streets. The tales are, however, no different when they are embedded within a society that prizes the rich and disparages and disenfranchises the poor. The rich and heirs to power are always welcome; the poor and wretched are cast out from the very beginning to live on the margins, to live on their wits and (at times) good fortune: "In the ancient city of London, on a certain autumn day in the second quarter of the sixteenth century, a boy was born to a poor family of the name of Canty, who did not want him. On the same day another English child was born to a rich family of the name of Tudor, who did want him. All England wanted him, too." Such predetermination can only prepare for the onslaught of unfairness, or the embrace of the gods.

And it is in London that Clemens begins the novel: "London was fifteen hundred years old, and was a great town—for that day. It had a hundred thousand inhabitants—some think double as many. The streets were very narrow, and crooked, and dirty, especially the part where Tom Canty lived, which was not far from London Bridge. . . . The house which Tom's father lived in was up a foul little pocket called Offal Court, out of Pudding Lane. It was small, decayed, and rickety, but it was packed full of wretchedly poor families."[2] A decade later, Jacob Riis would describe the tenements of New York and underscore the ubiquitous poverty and degradation. Tenement conditions had not changed so greatly over time, and it is probable that Clemens' familiarity with New York in the 1870s extended to the reality of its areas of grinding poverty. In *How the Other Half Lives*, Riis leads his reader into the darkness of a Cherry Street tenement:

> Be a little careful, please! The hall is dark and you might stumble over the children pitching pennies back there. Not that it would hurt them; kicks and cufs are their daily diet. They have little else. . . . Listen! That short hacking cough, that tiny, helpless wait—what do they mean? They mean that the soiled bow of white you saw on the door downstairs will have another story to tell—Oh! a sadly familiar story—before the day is at an end. The child is dying with measles. With half a chance it might have lived; but it had none. That dark bedroom killed it. . . . Come over here. Step carefully over this baby—it is a baby, spite of its rags and dirt—under these iron bridges called fire-escapes, but loaded down, despite the incessant watchfulness of the firemen, with broken household goods, with washtubs and barrels, over which no man could climb from a fire. The gap between dingy brick-walls is the yard. That strip of smoke-colored sky up there is the heaven of these people. Do you wonder the name does not attract them to the churches?[3]

Clemens' description of the Canty home aligns with Riis' descriptions: "Canty's tribe occupied a room on the third floor. The mother and father had a sort of bedstead in the corner; but Tom, his grandmother, and his two sisters, Bet and Nan, were not restricted—they had all the floor to themselves and might sleep where they chose. There were the remains of a blanket or two and some bundles of ancient and dirty straw, but these could not rightly be called beds, for they were not organized; they were kicked into a general pile mornings, and selections made from the mass at night for service" (4). The reality of the Canty's lives is shaped by absolute poverty and the resulting reliance on theft and beggary. Tom's father and grandmother alike have turned to drink to lessen their pain, though the combination of alcohol and poverty has made them, as it made Pap Finn, brutish abusers of the rest of the family. Here is a scene of the domestic side of hell, made more excruciating by the combination of frustration and resentment. Riis would comment, "The gap that separates the man with the patched coat from his wealthy neighbor is, after all, perhaps but a tenement."[4]

Clemens' novel strives to explore the distinction between wealth and poverty, between silk and patches. There are, in essence, two stories within the pages of the novel, and they are antithetical in intent and result. The first is the story of Tom Canty, his life, his dream of riches, and his attempt to conform to the conventions of wealth once he has changed clothes with Edward and is thought by the nobility to be the unbalanced prince. This is the story of the American Dream transplanted to Tudor England, a story prompted by but even more stirring than the Horatio Alger tales of hard work as an entrée into the middle class. Unlike Alger's Ragged Dicks who are recognized for some ambition and rewarded for their discipline with advance into a clerk's position, Tom is yanked out of his squalor by his ears by a playful Providence (or a somewhat interfering omniscient narrator) and dropped on the throne of England. It is the supreme domestic situation, this time with an ailing father (Henry VIII) who seeks only to save his distracted son so that the family can continue to shape its legacy. The fact that the situation is a bow to paternal wishes (as well as to class dominance) does not diminish the impact of the domestic scene: The concerned father here seeks desperately to protect his addled child, a long-standing sentimental construction of parent/child dependence. For Tom the situation presents not only the possibility of unbounded wealth but also, at its most basic, protection and comfort, two of the things he most craves when at the hands of his raging and violent father.

That comfort, in fact, undermines the dramatic tension in Tom's story because while he may be uncomfortable and uneasy about being found an imposter, the whole of Henry's household is working for his benefit and ease. Tom's experiences, while at times stressful, are not life threatening, and he is able to use his intuition and intelligence to adapt to the ways of court. The anxiety here is nothing like the stress that Tom experiences when he is at the mercy of his drunk father and grandmother. He is safe, and those around him wish him to remain safe, which lends little drama to his predicament. And in the end, Tom is the beneficiary of the King's (this time Edward VI's) affection and protection. His rise is assured and his family (his mother and sisters) is safe.

Adapting to wealth (as Clemens would show in a more complicated way in *The Tragedy of Pudd'nhead Wilson*) may have its corrupting influence; however, when a person of wealth and privilege finds himself deprived of comfort and cast down among the lower economic and social classes, there is a great deal more threat. Physical discomfort and danger are worries for the dispossessed, and they are Edward's worries after he is flung into poverty and forced to make his way among thieves and beggars. Growing up in privilege has set Edward's expectations for personal comfort and, perhaps more importantly, loyalty. The lack of both will, ultimately, have a profound effect on the young prince, though initially he is impatient and unreasonable in his expectation that commoners will be drawn to his complaints and concerned for his welfare. It is a perfect case of class blindness and the egocentrism at the foundation of nobility. Edward has no experience of his wishes being ignored and his person being violated. In fact, the easy environment of the King's household, populated as it is with the solicitous and obsequious, schools Edward in bias and disinterest. In a clear example of Edward's protection from discomfort, he is used to having the whipping boy take punishment (and used to getting the boy's gratitude for having the position to support his and his family's needs, which is very different from Tom's shock at that very idea). Edward is severely tested (and no doubt more than a little surprised) when John Canty beats him with impunity. Unlike the palace's preoccupation with protecting the supposedly insane prince, Offal Court (and later the camp of thieves) is a decidedly dangerous environment for the lucid and prickly Edward.

Before Edward's education in compassion can begin, however, he must face the dark side of Offal Court's domesticity. While we are introduced to the pain that Tom Canty suffers at the hands of his wild parent in the early portion of the story, John Canty becomes even more violent and mean-spirited in his dealings with Edward. In this way, Edward faces the hard lessons of moving from privilege to pain, a much more exacting lesson than Tom's movement toward comfort. We see this in Canty's Pap-like rant as he finds Edward in the street: "Out to this time of night again, and hast not brought a farthing home, I warrant me! If it be so, an' I do not break off the bones in they lean body, then I am not John Canty, but some other" (24). In response to Edward's plea to be taken home to the King, Canty warns the supposedly distracted child, "Gone stark mad as any Tom o' Bedlam! . . . But mad or no mad, I and thy Grammer Canty will soon find where the soft pieces in thy bones lie, or I'm no true man!" (24).

John Canty is kin to the brutish Pap, and the home he rules so violently presents the backstory that is missing from Huckleberry Finn's biography in both *The Adventures of Tom Sawyer* and its sequel. That backstory is the focus of chapter 10, which is placed after a brief aside to the palace to check on Tom and to juxtapose the mild and deferential treatment for the faux prince to the brutality aimed at Edward. The chapter opens as Canty beats back an attempt by Father Andrew to save the boy from his wrath, a warning to those who would infringe on his paternal rights (the priest's death will cause Canty to run from the authorities and give Edward his first chance to escape). Once "home" Edward takes stock of the dingy and offensive quarters, a room that has all the markings of a shanty: "Presently the prince found himself in John Canty's abode, with door closed against the outsiders. By the vague light of a tallow candle which was thrust into a bottle, he made out the main features of the loathsome den, and also the occupants of it. Two frowsy girls and a middle-aged woman cowered against the wall, in one corner, with the aspect of animals habituated to harsh usage and expecting and dreading it now. From another corner stole a withered hag with streaming gray hair and malignant eyes" (60). Here we see the Canty's distinct tie to Pap: The Canty grandam, with her "streaming" hair and "malignant eyes," offers a family resemblance to the adult Finn; the cowering woman and daughters present an uncompromised image of domestic abuse and recapitulate the dire environment of the forest cabin where Huck is kept prisoner by his father.

Through the rest of the chapter, readers are presented with the quiet attempts that a mother makes to resolve the mystery of her ailing child. Goodwife Canty, terrified for herself, her daughters, and her son, begs him to recant his claim that he is the prince because his words "be freighted with death for thee, and ruin for all that be near to thee" (61). Both sisters desperately plead with their father to leave the boy alone, a plea that works only when Bet hits on the possibility of the next day's earnings: "Tomorrow he will be himself again, and will beg with diligence and come not empty home again" (62). A moment of ease ends when Edward repeats that he is Henry's son; John Canty flies into a frenzy: "A sounding blow upon the prince's shoulder from Canty's broad palm, sent him staggering into Goodwife

Canty's arms, who clasped him to her breast and sheltered him from a pelting rain of cuffs and slaps by interposing her own person. The frightened girls retreated to their corners, but the grandmother stepped eagerly forward to assist her son." When Edward attempts to separate from her protection and again insists he is not Tom, "This speech infuriated the swine to such a degree that they set about their work without waste of time. Between them they belabored the boy right soundly, and then gave the girls and their mother a beating for showing sympathy for the victim" (63). The evening is one long violent dance, a dance that is answered by a death-defying sympathy as the mother tests Edward's reactions to see whether there is anything to his claim of sanity. The whole of this scene helps not only to explain Tom's befuddled notions about family and comfort during his time at the palace but also, and more importantly, to begin the lessons that later shape Edward VI. Those lessons are invariably domestic and are highlighted by situations of (most often) mothers and children. With both Huck and Edward there is a clear fascination with the maternal impulse and what might happen should that impulse be directed rightly and with affection.

In a variation of the biblical stricture that the first shall be made last, Edward's every move carries with it not only the guarantee of derision (the crowd is entertained by the rant; the thieves crown him "King Foo-Foo the First") but also the possibility of physical harm and the prospect of an early and difficult death. These dangers alone, however, do not lend themselves to the lessons of compassion; it is not enough that Edward is cast out of the palace and forced to move among commoners. The lessons that lead to compassion are possible only when they are presented in the company of honorable strangers who aid the infirm (perhaps Clemens' version of the parable of the Good Samaritan). For Edward, the hope for comfort and safety comes finally at the hands of the displaced Miles Hendon, who, despite the loss of ancestral halls and wealth and privilege (a hint here of the Robin Hood legend played at so deftly by Tom Sawyer and Joe Harper), stands at the side of the young boy and sees him through his earthly Valley of the Shadow of Death, though he is too late to save him from the deranged monk who claims to do archangel's work of retribution for Henry VIII's nationalizing Roman Catholic holdings; instead, Edward is "saved" by the tramp Hugo and John Canty, who spirit him away from the hermitage.

Before all that, however, Edward finds himself in the quieter atmosphere of the peasant woman and her two daughters, an atmosphere that Clemens knew full well as he looked at his own life and hearth and the presence of Livy, Susy, and Clara (Jean wasn't born until 1880 and may not have yet been a full character for Clemens;

in a similar way, he dedicates the novel to Susy and Clara, though Jean has been born into the family prior to the novel's publication). Clemens is looking at the impact of small acts of kindness. He describes Edward's entry into basic domestic scenes and, especially during Edward's solitary journey through the countryside, sets up situations within which the young prince is introduced to the virtue of compassion by way of familial ties and the love of mothers for children (this is similar to the lesson in the still-to-come Hank Morgan's and Arthur's journey when the King enters the smallpox hut to bring out the dying daughter so that the mother can hold her child). In this instance, Edward is first schooled in the simple pleasure of warmth and comfort. His first teacher, of course, is a calf. The passage is worth quoting at length:

> The king was not only delighted to find that the creature was only a calf, but delighted to have the calf's company; for he had been feeling so lonesome and friendless that the company and comradeship of even this humble animal was welcome. And he had been so buffeted, so rudely entreated by his own kind, that it was a real comfort to him to feel that he was at last in the society of a fellow creature that had at least a soft heart and a gentle spirit, whatever loftier attributes might be lacking. So he resolved to waive rank and make friends with the calf.
>
> While stroking its sleek warm back—for it lay near him and within easy reach—it occurred to him that this calf might be utilized in more ways than one. Whereupon he re-arranged his bed, spreading it down close to the calf; then he cuddled himself up to the calf's back, drew the covers up over himself and his friend, and in a minute or two was as warm and comfortable as he had ever been in the downy couches of the regal palace at Westminster.
>
> Pleasant thoughts came, at once, life took on a cheerfuller seeming. He was free of the bonds of servitude and crime, free of the companionship of base and brutal outlaws; he was warm, he was sheltered; in a word, he was happy. . . . He merely snuggled closer to his friend, in a luxury of warm contentment, and drifted blissfully out of consciousness into a deep and dreamless sleep that was full of serenity and peace. The distant dogs howled, the melancholy kine complained, and the winds went on raging, whilst the furious sheets of rain drove along the roof; but the majesty of England slept on, undisturbed, and the calf did the same, it being a simple creature and not easily troubled by storms or embarrassed by sleeping with a king. (158)

The tone of this passage is decidedly calm, especially in comparison to the scenes immediately preceding that describe Edward's experience among the thieves and his first experience with the suffering caused by Henry's laws. Edward's sense of loss and his tender thoughts sparked by the image of his father as "father" and not "king" are torn asunder by the Ruffler's memorial to Black Bess and by accounts of the punishments handed out by law. Eulogizing Black Bess, Ruffler opines: "Her gift of palmistry and other sorts of fortune-telling begot for her at last a witch's name and fame. The law roasted her to death at a slow fire. It did touch me to a story of tenderness to see the gallant way she met her lot—cursing and reviling all the crowd that gaped and gazed around her, whilst the flames licked upward toward her face and catched her thin locks and crackled about her old gray head—cursing them, said I?—cursing them! why an' thou shouldst live a thousand years thou'dst never hear so masterful cursing. Alack, her art died with her. There be base and weakling imitations left, but no true blasphemy" (142). Witnessing such common and aggressive feeling is a new experience for the prince, and he is at first unable to fathom the contradiction between his assumptions of courtly compassion and the evidence of oppression and the foul result of enforcing laws. Here is a group of commoners whose bond is their shared ill treatment by the existing law and whose energy and language is devoted not to a chivalrous fealty to Henry but to creating new and effective curses against the King, curses that are prized and appreciated all the more for having been spewed at the moment of death. That energy, however, dissipates as their number dwindles and they are deprived of their rude poetry. This is not his father's household, which is made most clear during the mock coronation that makes ridiculous Edward's claim to nobility and underscores the distance he has fallen and the tramps' aggressive challenge to the House of Tudor.

In contrast to the emotional vertigo induced during Edward's time with the rabble, his night spent with the calf allows him a small sense of peace and its warmth, a genuine and physical sensation, makes it possible for him to understand authentic and uncomplicated comfort. In place of the rough politics of class division is the simplicity of the barn and the rest of solitude that allows refuge in the face of storms both natural and man-made. The lesson is that it is possible to find rest away from the blunderbuss of political and economic competition that pits man against man for the most basic of human needs. Children and calves are the teachers of humility: They dispense peace. The Clemens girls would be especially pleased that the lesson is taught by one of their favorite animals.

The scene with the calf leads immediately to Edward's confrontation with the two young peasant girls. If comfort is possible when one sets aside the cares of the crown, here Edward is taught the value of authentic compassion and the importance of simple acceptance. There is no larger agenda that prevents the children from accepting Edward at face value, and their strong moral fiber only convinces them of his truthfulness: "Would he say a lie? For look you, Prissy, an' it were not true, it *would* be a lie. It surely would be. Now think on't. For all things that be not true, be lies—thou canst make naught else out of it" (161). Embraced by the girls, Edward muses: "When I am come to mine own again, I will always honor little children, remembering how these trusted me and believed in me in my time of trouble, whilst they that were older, and thought themselves wiser, mocked at me and held me for a liar" (161).

The girls' mother is one of those rare individuals in Edwards' experience that prize true sentiment. We are told, "The children's mother received the king kindly, and was full of pity; for his forlorn condition and apparently crazed intellect touched her womanly heart. She was a widow, and rather poor; consequently, she had seen trouble enough to enable her to feel for the unfortunate" (162). She is aligned with Goodwife Canty and Miles Hendon in her willingness to open her home and her heart to the child. Clemens here uses this most recent member of the trilogy of sympathy to drive his ideal of social responsibility. The genealogy of sympathy in Clemens' novels here extends backward to Aunt Polly, the Widow Douglas, and Jim. At this moment, the peasant mother is linked to the earlier characters who give of themselves when presented with the specter of a child in trouble. We see, then, that while the collection of characters emphasizes a woman's role in extending aid, it is also clear that Clemens alludes to a much more inclusive notion of sympathy: It is male and female; it is black and white.

4

A Connecticut Yankee in King Arthur's Household and the Tragedy of Valet de Chambre

> I seemed to have flown back out of that age into this of ours, and then forward to it again, and was set down, a stranger and forlorn in that strange England, with an abyss of thirteen centuries yawning between me and you! between me and my home and my friends! between me and all that is dear to me, all that could make life worth the living!
>
> —*A Connecticut Yankee in King Arthur's Court*

As Clemens approached his second English novel, he returned to the trope of the hero looking back at the sweep of his experience. When did Hank Morgan find the time to write his manuscript? Hank in his way is very much like Huck Finn: Both have time to fill as they wait for the outcome of their final episode. For Huck, waiting to see how Tom Sawyer healed from his wound before he launches again into the territories, finds time to write his book while chafing against Aunt Sally's civilizing. Hank, amid the destruction and waste of his failed republic, and perhaps more importantly, amid the wreckage of his domestic life, turns to tell the story of how he found bliss not from the political power of "the boss" but from the domestic care of wife and child. Both narrators must come to terms with their life choices; both must find meaning that will help them gain peace. Huck's peace is at best fleeting and will only lead him off to other adventures and, most likely, an early death. Hank's peace is profound and is gained with the verbal resurrection of his "family" and friends just as he slips into death.

While readers often find Hank's story troubling, scholars too easily deflect the heart-felt anxiety toward Hank into neatly ordered commentaries on social and political force. Clemens' rage in *A Connecticut Yankee* is often ascribed to his interest in and commitment to justice—both political/institutional and racial—or to the chaos of his life in the late 1880s as financial worries over the Paige typesetter and/or the Charles L. Webster company took a stranglehold. That is too simple a reading. We have gilded Sam Clemens as social sage and anti-imperialist champion and have been deliberate about and very successful at installing that image of him as a part of U.S. cultural iconography. But we have ignored the heartbreak that is at the center of Hank's motivation for his woeful tale.

Demonizing Hank Morgan as a self-deluded confidence man also makes critics feel better about ourselves and reinforces our own superiority as we correct (that is, analyze and therefore diminish) the potential for sympathy formed in the maelstrom of readers' emotions. Reading Hank as ironic has been key: Irony sets up intellectual distance and suggests that Hank is a tool for Clemens' social and political criticism. The pain in the story is diffused when it is seemingly sparked by general human foolishness (Hank as representative type), and the tale stands as a parable of hubris rather than an exploration of a tortured soul. More important, and more to my purpose here, is the critical blindness to the deeply personal pain that forms the center of this novel. Many critics fail to understand (or choose to ignore) that at the heart of literary work is emotional recognition. But what do we recognize in Hank Morgan? What possibility for sympathy exists for a character that so deliberately refuses to admit his complicity in oppression and his particularly potent (perhaps even virulent) tendency toward violence and despair.

Hank is in psychological distress. Hank is, in fact, insane. At the opening of his story, in the third sentence of the tale, there is a suggestion that Hank has landed in an asylum. Facing Sir Kay, Hank contemplates the news that he is outside of Camelot: "CAMELOT—Camelot. . . . I don't seem to remember hearing of it before. Name of the asylum, likely" (9). When he first meets Clarence, Hank asks, "And this isn't an asylum? I mean, it isn't a place where they cure crazy people?" (14). Moments later, Hank reverts to his "Yankee" pragmatism and pledges, "If it was still the nineteenth century and I was among lunatics and couldn't get away, I would presently boss that asylum or know the reason why" (15). These seemingly throwaway comments deserve more respect. Hank is methodical and disciplined in his writing. He tells Mark Twain, "First, I kept a journal; then by and by, after years, I took the journal and turned it into a book" (8). In his writing Hank attempts to recreate a world for himself, a world that still has the potential for the human connection he once had with his family and his friends. The reality of this, however, is that he is unable to reintegrate his emotional life: The resulting chaos at the penultimate horror of the Battle of the Sand Belt is the manifestation of a conscience at war. Hank is no longer able to hide behind arrogance and mechanical and political ingenuity. And he can no longer ignore or deny the depth of his own misery. His attempt to shy away from loss only reinforces his emptiness.

Sandy and Hello Central are key. At the end of his narrative, Hank flashes to life at the memory of his wife and his child. Their memory punctuates the final scene when Hank's voice takes over from the voyeur Mark Twain and echoes strongly through the bedchamber already under the pall of death:

> O, Sandy, you are come at last,—how I have longed for you! Sit by me—do not leave me—never leave me again, Sandy, never again. Where is your hand?—give it me, dear, let me hold it—there—now, all is well, all is peace, and I am happy again—*we* are happy again, isn't it so, Sandy? You are so dim, so vague, you are but a mist, a cloud, but are *here*, and that is blessedness sufficient; and I have your hand; don't take it away—it is only for a little while, I shall not require it long. . . . Was that the child? . . . Hello Central! . . . She doesn't answer. Asleep, perhaps? Bring her when she wakes, and let me touch her hands, her face, her hair, and tell her good-bye. . . . Sandy! . . . Yes, you are there. I lost myself a moment, and I thought you were gone. . . . Have I been sick long? It must be so; it seems months to me. And such dreams! such strange and awful dreams, Sandy! Dreams that were as real as reality—delirium, of course, but *so* real! Why, I thought the king was dead, I thought you were in Gaul and couldn't get home, I thought there was a revolution; in the fantastic frenzy of these dreams, I thought that Clarence and I, and a handful of my cadets fought and exterminated the whole chivalry of England! But even that was not the strangest. I seemed to be a creature of a remote unborn age, centuries hence, and even *that* was as real as the rest! Yes, I seemed to have flown back out of that age into this of ours, and then forward to it again, and was set down, a stranger and forlorn in that strange England, with an abyss of thirteen centuries yawning between

> me and you! between me and my home and my friends! between me and all that is dear to me, all that could make life worth the living! It was awful—awfuler than you can ever imagine, Sandy. Ah, watch by me, Sandy—stay by me every moment—*don't* let me go out of my mind again; death is nothing, let it come, but not with those dreams, not with the torture of those hideous dreams—I cannot endure *that* again. . . . Sandy? (432)

"Mark Twain," the frame narrator and audience for Hank's tale, fails to understand in the end that it was the story and its focus on building and then losing relationships and not the "effect" that drew Hank out of himself and into a concern for the world. Hank Morgan's autobiography comes alive when we take an interpretive leap and sympathize with the bereaved and exiled and insane Yankee.

While the novel may have taken root in Clemens' imagination fairly early and with a predictable interest in the comedy of a medieval knight frantically trying to get comfortable in his suit of armor or in the suggestion of George Washington Cable that Clemens become familiar with *Le Morte d'Arthur*, the story clearly evolved differently once Clemens began to put pen to paper. Even the early chapters that most clearly mimic Mallory's epic turn to a very different axis as Hank falls into his conscience-driven tale. The tale is a potent mix of classic romance and nineteenth-century American realism, and like Huck Finn, who ultimately challenges Tom Sawyer's imagination to come to understand the workings of the real world, Hank finds himself at first captive in an alien community.

Perhaps it is better to back into this discussion. When Mark Twain encounters Hank Morgan for the first time, this is how we see the Yankee:

> It was in Warwick Castle that I came across the curious stranger whom I am going to talk about. . . . As he talked along, softly, pleasantly, flowingly, he seemed to drift away imperceptibly out of this world and time, and into some remote era and old forgotten country; and so he gradually wove such a spell about me that I seemed to move among the specters and shadows and dust and mold of a gray antiquity, holding speech with a relic of it! Exactly as I would speak of my nearest personal friends or enemies, or my most familiar neighbors, he spoke of Sir Bedivere, Sir Bors of Ganis, Sir Lancelot of the Lake, Sir Galahad, and all the other great names of the Table Round—and how old, old, unspeakably old and faded and dry and musty and ancient he came to look as he went on! Presently he turned to me and said, just as one might speak of the weather or any other common matter—

"You know about transmigration of souls; do you know about transposition of epochs—and bodies?" (2)

As the tale moves on, Mark Twain becomes the reader of Hank Morgan's text, a text that clearly demands an introductory "He says" to set Hank's tale apart and to emphasize Hank's voice as teller and interpreter.

Hank is in deep trouble. He is desperate because of an unquenchable loss. He has experienced death firsthand and feels guilt for having survived. Hank is marked with the guilt of the survivor. His conscience is his enemy. He writes:

> If I had the remaking of man, he wouldn't have any conscience. It is one of the most disagreeable things connected with a person; and although it certainly does a great deal of good, it cannot be said to pay, in the long run; it would be much better to have less good and more comfort. . . . I have noticed my conscience for many years, and I know it is more trouble and bother to me than anything else I started with. I suppose that in the beginning I prized it, because we prize anything that is ours; and yet how foolish it was to think so. If we look at it another way, we see how absurd it is: if I had an anvil in me would I prize it? Of course not. And yet when you come to think, there is no real difference between a conscience and an anvil—I mean for comfort. I have noticed it a thousand times. And you could dissolve an anvil with acids, when you couldn't stand it any longer; but there isn't any way you can work off a conscience—at least so it will stay worked off; not that I know of, anyway. (146)

One way that Hank attempts to "work off" his conscience is to convince himself that man is the product of his training. Training driven to the extreme removes the need of reflection and regret (though there is still the nagging worry of redemption). The most heinous crimes, the most troublesome memory is washed clean once you believe that there is no power—physical or moral—that challenges training. In one of the more often-quoted passages, Hank explains away the possibility of human responsibility:

> Training—training is everything; training is all there is *to* a person. We speak of nature; it is folly; there is no such thing as nature; what we call by that misleading name is merely heredity and training. We have no thoughts of our own, no opinions of our own; they are transmitted to us, trained into us. All that is original in us, and therefore fairly creditable or

> discreditable to us, can be covered up and hidden by the point of a cambric needle, all the rest being atoms contributed by, and inherited from, a procession of ancestors that stretches back a billion years to the Adam-clam or grasshopper or monkey from whom our race has been so tediously and ostentatiously and unprofitably developed. And as for me, all that I think about in this plodding pilgrimage, this pathetic drift between the eternities, is to look out and humbly live a pure and high and blameless life, and save that one microscopic atom in me that is truly *me*: the rest may land in Sheol and welcome for all I care. (143)

But what has prompted Hank's crisis? Why does he seek dispensation and the rest of the conscienceless? What turns hope to dross? Compassion to steel?

Hank's chaotic slide into cynicism and despair is the result of losing his wife and child. We are not told of that loss until the end of his tale, but it overhangs the whole of his manuscript and is, I think, the primary reason for his unease: The emotional center of the tale is Hank's gradual softening from hard-hearted Yankee to devoted husband and father (a shift that mimics Clemens' own history during the 1870s and 1880s). At the end, Hank is crushed not by his loss of Camelot or England but by his loss of Sandy and Hello Central (a prophetic tale that presages Clemens' own despair). His story—told as reminiscence seasoned with the images of loss—is an attempt to reclaim an emotional connection to the past and to those he has left, those who have left him, or those who have been taken from him.

When we reflect on the whole of Hank's story, the most emotionally charged scenes involve parents and children, often ending with the deaths of both. One disturbing reality here is that parents are often unable to protect their children from brutality: the multiple scenes of slave gangs, the beating of a mother whose child is taken from her grasp. In a way, Hank's "man factories" are an attempt to answer the institutional threat to families (think of his stepping in to save Hugo from the Queen's dungeon). He travels through the kingdom, confronts the fact of helplessness, and attempts to save the family by making it possible for spouses and parents to stand against social and political forces.

Perhaps no episode is as filled with sentiment as Arthur's unabashed courage as he carries a peasant woman's dying daughter from the smallpox hut. Hank stands in awe and is struck with the juxtaposition of his own self-image as "boss," an image that contrasts his intellectual and mechanical acumen and power, which is noticeably lacking in genuine heart-felt compassion, with Arthur's bearing and compassion: "He came forward into the light; upon his breast lay a slender girl of fifteen.

She was all but half conscious; she was dying of smallpox. Here was heroism at its last and loftiest possibility, its utmost summit; this was challenging death in the open field unarmed, with all the odds against the challenger, no reward set upon the contest, and no admiring world in silks and cloth of gold to gaze and applaud; and yet the king's bearing was as serenely brave as it had always been in those cheaper contests where knight meets knight in equal fight and clothed in protecting steel. He was great now; sublimely great" (274). Arthur here is the manifestation of masculine emotional power. Hank does not measure up. He has spent his time, in fact, running away from any real emotion. His behavior toward Sandy demonstrates his uncertainty and his inability to confront genuine affection, at least initially. Overall, we might argue that Hank is trying throughout his tale to ignore his emotions. By the time he tells the whole story, he has accepted, embraced, and then lost his opportunity for human affection. All that is left in the end is to repress, to deny.

Clemens' Hank Morgan is an exceedingly complex man who struggles against myriad personal demons. While those demons are enlivened by ethnocentrism and imperialist beliefs, they are fueled especially by Hank's aloneness. Sandy and Hello Central figure prominently in the closing scene as Hank loses his tenuous hold on sanity and falls into a deep despair. In bed and facing (and embracing) death, Hank finally is forced to peel away the layers of denial and confront the genuine loss that is the center of his emotional life. Hank dies knowing what is more important. It is not physical or technological prowess; it is not profit; it is not power. It is human companionship; it is compassion; it is recognition that we cannot live alone.

A Connecticut Yankee, though it ends with a death, offers readers a look at Hank's attempt to find salvation in human companionship: Hank is more human because of his companions (Clarence, Arthur, Sandy); Mark Twain is more human because of Hank's reaching out to him. However, Hank's bid for salvation is finally swamped by personal, emotional chaos. Clemens, always the master of misdirection, insists on a final word. The narrator Mark Twain misses the lesson and does not reach back to Hank. With the death rattle in his throat, the Yankee finds his voice: "A bugle? . . . It is the king! The drawbridge, there! Man the battlements—turn out the . . . ." Death takes Hank. And Twain's final comment? "He was getting up his last 'effect'; but he never finished it" (433). Perhaps in the end, the reality of loss was too heavy for the frail mind, and it yet again let in the chaos. The final "effect" is never the point: Hank's death throes do not mitigate the sentiment in his plea. There is small satisfaction in the cold mechanics of the effect, and it is a false comfort and a cheat.

The financial pressures on Clemens mounted during the late 1880s and early 1890s. Already he had funneled thousands of dollars into the ill-fated Paige typesetting machine. More troubling, he had begun to shift funds out of the Webster company, which ultimately led to the ruin of that company and of Clemens' Colonel Sellers–like dream of unlimited wealth. The financial burden was acute, and in 1890 the Clemenses packed up and headed for Europe, hoping that the change would lessen the stress on their budget. From 1890 to 1894, Clemens became a vagabond businessman as he shuttled back and forth to keep a hand in business and seemingly to push Paige to some success. That never did happen, and in 1894, Clemens was forced to declare bankruptcy to protect his family. Only the machinations of Henry H. Rogers saved Clemens from losing his most valuable possession—his copyrights. Rogers was able to negotiate that Olivia Clemens was a primary creditor (because Clemens had used portions of Livy's own fortune to bankroll his investments). Clemens was bound to Rogers from that day on, and he was elaborately appreciative of Rogers' business skills, skills that Clemens sorely wished he had.

When Clemens finished *The Adventures of Tom Sawyer*, he saw his boy claim a future of professional and domestic bliss—or so we are made to think. Tom is rich; Judge Thatcher has taken him under his wing to make sure that he will move in proper circles, though by *Adventures of Huckleberry Finn* only the stagnant wealth remains: Becky, the Judge, even Aunt Polly are gone from the scene, and Tom has resorted to bullying both Huck and, this time, Jim as a way to reinforce his personal status. In the years to come, Tom grows but also falls victim to unrealized (and perhaps unrealizable) expectations. What begins as a celebration of conventionality morphs into the embrace of racialist thinking and later into a view of the underbelly of classist and racist thought and custom. If we were to look forward from 1876 we might see Tom as a young lawyer making his way into new territory. He would, however, be hampered by a residue of humor and a penchant for the new and the odd invention. David Wilson is the end point of Tom Sawyer's adult future.

Wilson's welcome at Dawson's Landing is a disaster. His interest in the mystery of the town's robberies and his collecting of fingerprints point to a young man uncomfortable with the demands of adult social life. He lives off his fortune (readers are often perplexed by Wilson's ability to live when he is so clearly unable to find any acceptable work); he is a dilettante and a dabbler. Most importantly, he believes in the social hierarchy; his relationship with Judge Driscoll is an echo of Tom's childhood tie with Judge Thatcher, and the "free thinking" Judge is, in reality, a stodgy and class-bound patriarch who is more concerned with reputation, honor, and blood. Wilson, though, feels completely at home in the close atmosphere of Driscoll's shadow and finds comfort as the Judge's single "freethinking" companion. The reality, of course, is that neither Driscoll nor Wilson is a free thinker and each is bound to the severe political space of Dawson's Landing. The domestic scene is highlighted not by a full embrace of individual humanity but by the absolute foundation of the slave system that undergirds the town's economic, political, and social life.

By the time of *The Tragedy of Pudd'nhead Wilson*, Clemens had seen the danger in an early success based on shallowness and rigid conservatism. What underscores Wilson's (and in imagination Tom's) bow to social order is his role in supporting and reinscribing slavery. It is not enough for him to find the killer of his friend and supporter. He must reclaim and reconstitute the system to which the Judge dedicated his life and that has been the focal point for Wilson's own life. If Roxy upsets the natural order when she changes the babies—turning white into black and black into white—Wilson is the avenging angel who puts things right. His success, marginal and weak as it is in the end, is that he confirms the town's social order and delivers retribution for the attack on slavery. If Roxy turns the world upside down, Wilson brings it back to its proper axis and orbit. He destroys the town by saving it—the true tragedy of the novel.

In *Pudd'nhead Wilson* Samuel Clemens returned to the formula that had worked so well in the past. The novel uses the primary trope of competing "twins" to set up the internal domestic battle. It's quite likely that, like the shifting of Tom Canty and Edward VI, the switch of Thomas Driscoll and Valet de Chambre (Chambers) is a fall back to the question of what to do when an individual finds himself awash with wealth and in a stable household but unable to appreciate or understand that blessing. Throughout the novels written during his major phase, Clemens focuses his attention on the plight of the heretofore disenfranchised child who must navigate a more or less intact household tuned to the needs of its members. The issue is at the heart of Huckleberry Finn's wandering and is highlighted by his contact with the Widow Douglas, Judith Loftus, the Wilkes sisters, and the Phelps family. At each domestic stop, Huck is forced to take stock of his expectations of domestic life and to come to some decision about whether he is willing to accept physical (and perhaps spiritual) safety by facing demons, his as well as others'.

Safety is the heart of Roxy's act of rebellion. Her decision to switch her child with her master's son comes at the end of a tortuous process that leads her from absolute despair to a kind of manic embrace of the possibility that Chambers can be saved. Returning to the trope of twins that formed the spine of *The Prince and the Pauper*, Clemens has Roxy recognize that the two babies (one the pure blood child of her master; the other the hybrid of white and black born of her relation with Essex) are, for all intents and purposes, doubles. Roxy is astute enough (and also coldhearted enough) to switch the boys. For her there is no second-guessing or tortured reflection. If she wants her child to live, she must (she thinks irrevocably) exchange the children's identities; and more, she must give up her own relationship with her son to reinforce his newly acquired position as the heir to the Driscoll family and as her master. This is a version of an absolute love of the mother for her child. At first willing to commit infanticide to keep her child by her side and out of the grips of slavery, she is now willing to let go of that child so that he may live, and live in comfort, and (she thinks) privilege, both physical and moral. The situation is abundantly domestic. Roxy gives up her true status as a mother in order to better the life of her child—a (perhaps) selfless act that defines the cult of motherhood.

The reality is a good deal more complicated: While she accepts her role as a slave, which means that she will have a hand in bringing up her son to believe in the absolute supremacy of white over black, Roxy also carries in her a satisfaction in his passing for white and in his exacting some retribution for crimes against their race. Revenge, though not an explicitly mentioned motivation, cannot be set aside as an underlying goal as Roxy contemplates the tectonic shift in her own life. This extends the battleground over slavery—and concurrently over race and identity—throughout the domestic sphere. Roxy, Chambers, and Tom present the focal point for Clemens' exploration of what it means to be identified by others who make the rules far from any notion of altruism. It's clear that Roxy emulates the practice of whites who have come together to define, describe, and set the terms for identity. What has been done to her and to hers is the model for her actions toward the powerless Tom Driscoll. She sees nothing immoral about robbing a child of his inheritance and, in fact, glories in the prospect of sending off Chambers to usurp the role of "master." In the realm of domestic politics, Roxy is a wily fighter who has been trained to think of the powerless as potential fodder for her and her son's efforts to assure a comfortable future.

Of course, the effort is doomed from the start (much like Hank Morgan's restructuring of Arthurian England or Tom Canty's rise to the kingship as the ersatz Edward VI). Clemens' decision to ground the novel in the domestic worries of a slave mother and child is testament to the continuing trauma of using race as a primary category in personal and community politics. Here the focus is not on the historical record of antebellum social demands but on the ongoing and troublesome questions of a post–Civil War and post-Reconstruction legacy of miscegenation. "Passing" and worry about the place of free and more lightly toned blacks were the focus for the work of several important African American writers. It is the main concern of Frances E. W. Harper's *Iola LeRoy* (1892) and would be the primary concern for Pauline Hopkins' *Contending Forces* (1900) and Charles Chesnutt's *The Marrow of Tradition* (1902). Harper's book is especially valuable here because of its plotline, which follows the life of a young woman whose manumitted mother is married to her "master" until his unanticipated death allows a cousin to sell mother and children (a daughter and a son) into slavery.

One of the main questions that Harper asks is whether it is better for a black person of light complexion to try to pass into white society or to claim allegiance with the whole of the black community. Harper's tale is set after the Civil War, and the novel bridges the periods of slavery and freedom and ultimately focuses on the debate over black devotion to the very idea of restoring those households that were dissolved during slavery, and especially to restoring the ties between slave mothers and their lost children. The politics of the novel clearly focus on reestablishing the black family as a social and spiritual force, which sets up the emphasis on domesticity by a generation of men and women affected by slavery. Iola struggles with that question of allegiance and ultimately ties her future to her mother's community, at one point refusing a proposal of marriage from a northern white physician. In Harper's novel, which uses a mix of sentimental conventions and a strong-voiced didacticism, the evils of slavery, while never erased, are mitigated as Iola's extended family (her mother, her brother, her uncle, and her grandmother) are reunited and as a new generation (Iola and her black physician husband, her brother, and his social reformer wife) take steps to return to the South to work for the welfare and progress of the black community.

Clemens' tale, however, has no such ambitions. It offers no possibility that Roxy will transcend her oppression, and it remains tightly constructed to highlight the dilemma of racial categories. Even the setting for Clemens' novel is pinched, dealing as it does with the small rural setting of Dawson's Landing and never looking beyond the close horizon, even if Chambers (as Tom) gets to travel east for his education or if the town is invaded by the Luigi twins, who, while supposedly tied to the Old World of Europe, seem more clearly related to the rascally tribe of conmen along the Mississippi (kin, it seems, to the Duke and the King rather than to any European nobility). Still, both Harper's and Clemens' novels take their cue from and shine a sharp spotlight on domestic relationships. And it is the history of miscegenation acted out within the plantation household that most clearly sets the stage for the destruction of individual lives—at least black lives.

One, perhaps uncanny, similarity is in the ways that both Iola and Roxy are described and the way the individual descriptions set their status in the eyes of others. For Iola, her appearance drives Dr. Gresham both to wonder at her beginnings and to be mightily attracted to her. When he spies her working among the wounded in a field hospital, he comments:

> She is one of the most refined and lady-like women I ever saw. I hear she is a refugee, but she does not look like the other refugees who have come into our camp. He accent is slightly Southern but her manner is Northern. She is self-respecting without being supercilious; quiet without being dull. Her voice is low and sweet; yet at times there are tones of such passionate tenderness in it that you would think some great sorrow has darkened and overshadowed her life. Without being the least gloomy, her face at times is pervaded by an air of inexpressible sadness. . . . When she smiles, there is longing in her eyes which is never satisfied. I cannot understand how a Southern lady, whose education and manners stamp her as a woman of fine culture and good breeding, could consent to occupy the position she so faithfully holds.[1]

Colonel Robinson answers the doctor's query very simply, "Miss Leroy was a slave." The doctor then exclaims, "Oh, no. . . . It can't be so! A woman as white as she a slave!"[2]

Roxy, however, has no sophistication in her tone or her manner. She is, though, presented with a similar sense of the unusual. Here, along with the assumption of whiteness, Clemens introduces the complexity of Roxy's language and manner:

> From Roxy's manner of speech, a stranger would have expected her to be black, but she was not. Only one sixteenth of her was black, and that sixteenth did not show. She was of majestic form and stature, her attitudes were imposing and statuesque, and her gestures and movements distinguished by a noble and stately grace. Her complexion was very fair, with the rosy glow of vigorous health in the cheeks, her face was full of character and expression, her eyes were brown and liquid, and she had a heavy suit of fine soft hair which was also brown. . . . Her face was shapely, intelligent, and comely—even beautiful. She had an easy, independent carriage—when she was among her own caste—and a high and "sassy" way, withal; but of

> course she was meek and humble enough where white people were.
>
> To all intents and purposes Roxy was as white as anybody, but the one sixteenth of her which was black outvoted the other fifteen parts and made her a negro. She was saleable as such.[3]

Her son is painted with a similar brush: "Her son was thirty-one parts white, and he, too, was a slave, and by a fiction of law and custom a negro."[4]

While each writer offers the description within the context of the social definitions of race and the expectations for (especially) black women, both writers place their characters firmly within the women's sphere. Iola is embedded in and defined by her status as a nurse to the wounded; Roxy is constrained within the kitchen, and her role as servant is never questioned. Obviously, Iola has a genuine opportunity to set aside her racial background because of the education that she received in the North, an education arranged by her father as a way to protect her from the social stigma of her mixed heritage. Roxy has never and would never have such an opportunity. Her brush with white power and the sophistication of the white household is only a result of her sexual liaison with Colonel Cecil Burleigh Essex, a member of the First Families of Virginia, who holds a privileged place in the small town. Iola will come to define her self-worth through her connection to the black community; she will also see that connection as morally upright and socially ennobling as she devotes herself to the cause of social justice in a post-Reconstruction South. Roxy too will define herself within the black community, but it is a community of slaves who are always at the call of owners or other whites. Her tie to Essex, tenuous and steeped in an ideology that casts her as wanton and inferior, carries a great deal more importance as she accepts the rule of biology as determinant in the character of her son, a clear case of the oppressed adopting the values and worldview of the oppressor. Iola's tale ends with the restoration of a black household that resonates with both political and social purpose. Roxy's tale ends in the complete destruction of her and her child's lives and the reconstitution of slavery as the primary social force in Dawson's Landing.

Both Harper and Clemens center the lives of their black characters in the relationship of parent to child; however, for Clemens that relationship, tainted by the ideology of servitude and ruled by both law and custom, holds no positive lesson, no positive result. Once Chambers becomes Tom, Clemens begins to develop a story about the weaknesses of a motherly bond that is overwhelmed by racist doctrine and twisted by desperation. In the opening lines of chapter 10, the morning after Roxy has revealed to Tom the secret of his racial identity, he suddenly awakens:

"'Oh, joy, it was all a dream!' Then he laid himself heavily down again, with a groan and the muttered words, 'A nigger! I am a nigger! Oh, I wish I was dead!'" (121). Tom accepts Roxy's truth because he has been indoctrinated with the fear of it throughout his privileged life. Ironically, Wilson has the same dream at the close of chapter 20. After pondering over a confusion of clues, he "slept through a troubled and unrestful hour, then unconsciousness began to shred away, and presently he rose drowsily to a sitting posture. 'Now what was that dream?' he said, trying to recall it. 'What was the dream? It seemed to unravel that puz—'" (277). In one fell swoop, Wilson realizes that Tom and Chambers were switched as infants, that Tom is in fact Chambers and legally a black man and a slave, that the unidentified girl who fled the scene of Judge Driscoll's murder was Tom in disguise, that Tom and not Luigi killed the judge, and that robbery and not revenge was his motive. Wilson is able to solve this series of mysteries because he imagines in his sleep the awful possibility, which, Twain suggests, was a fear common to Southerners at the time: that according to the "one drop rule" a "white" person's racial status may be changed overnight by the revelation of black ancestry, no matter how distant. Wilson saves the town, and is rewarded, by exposing the hypocrisy at the root of white(washed) society.

Put another way, *Pudd'nhead Wilson* examines white society's fear of the racial other and the reality of miscegenation. Tom's fear is every white man's. Twain is not interested in racial balance or passing per se but in the effect of white paranoia on the whole of society. The worry is that we are all black inside—the inversion of Huck's line about Jim. It's a question of how white society deals with and addresses its possible loss of status. Roxy's act of switching the babies in the nursery is ultimately the most dangerous threat imaginable to white power and authority.

Conclusion

Sam Clemens' Haunted Home

> Why did I build this house, two years ago? To shelter this
> vast emptiness? How foolish I was! But I shall stay in it.
> The spirits of the dead hallow a house, for me.
> —*Autobiography of Mark Twain*

THE FINAL DECADES of Sam Clemens' life were, to be frank, a mess. After his bankruptcy, a story that has been told long and often, the Clemenses' life could not be repaired. The death of Susy Clemens, in 1896, as Clemens came to the end of the world tour that was aimed at resurrecting his financial life was a severe and complete blow to the family's emotional integrity. The family went into mourning for roughly a year; and Sam and Livy faced an emptiness that they were never able to ease. Clara and Jean had an increasingly difficult time: Jean's diagnosis of epilepsy dealt yet another blow to the family; Clara would become a central actor in the domestic play and often served as an emotional lever as Livy's illnesses became more frequent and Sam became more emotionally distant, most often preoccupied with his earning back his fortune, considering his legacy and posthumous reputation, and the dire prospect of losing Livy. Clemens' domestic fictions during the final decade or so often focused on loss, and his writing became more a means toward seeking some kind of emotional reconciliation.

In the midst of the financial turmoil that reached a crescendo in 1894, Clemens turned to his writing to make a profit, a primary motivation for *Pudd'nhead Wilson* and the later Tom Sawyer sequels, *Tom Sawyer Abroad* and *Tom Sawyer, Detective*, as well as the purposely penned *Following the Equator*. The 1890s were shaped by financial pressures, and Clemens turned to his writing (and lecturing during the world tour of 1895–96) to regroup. Yet, even as the financial picture became more clear and more dour, Clemens chose to enter the atmosphere of spiritual martyrdom with *Personal Recollections of Joan of Arc* (1896). The book, a novelized history of Joan's childhood, military prowess, spiritual purity, and martyrdom, has been most often presented as an aberration in Clemens' canon; however, when placed within the context of the range of domestic fictions that are the heart of Clemens' work, the book takes on a force that, despite its aesthetic problems, affixes it as a central work in Clemens' later years.

Clemens began the book in 1894 and completed it in 1896. In *Joan* Clemens seemed much more interested in the relationship of his narrator, Sieur Louis de Conte, to the ideal Joan, a figure that gained resonance as a protestant saint more in her battles against the confines of Roman Catholicism's ritual and obstinacy than in her canonized identity as Roman Catholic saint. This is not the usual hagiography that ends in triumph and glory. For Clemens, Joan's image and iconoclastic (if not ecclesiastic) fire inspired a sense of triumph; however, telling the tale through de Conte's eyes enforces a deep and abiding sense of loss that is intensely personal for de Conte and has given depth and resonance to his long life. Joan's ability to marshal an army for a supreme nationalistic cause (the unification of France and the restoration of the monarchy) set her apart from the usual domestic heroine; however, through de Conte, we see that Joan's power, while decorated with military trappings, was innately feminine because of its focus on the restoration of moral virtue and the creation of a community bound by the rule of God. Joan establishes, at least for a time, an overriding focus on applying to a broad national stage the power present so readily in the intimate domestic sphere.

Joan is, in the end, betrayed by those who find her Christian faith suspect and who are more insistent and more interested in achieving and holding on to worldly power. Her martyrdom is foreordained and assured by a political and ecclesiastic system that prizes the certainty of separate spheres and fails to see the worth of an individual relationship to God. For the authorities, any relation to God must be mediated rather than immediate, and that necessity forms the base argument against the young warrior. She is not the typical realist hero, though her rejection of the dominant ideology and her skepticism toward the usual expressions of faith so ally her with Clemens' earlier outsider, Huck Finn. Joan is much more certain of her place in the moral scheme and never fails to challenge purposely and aggressively the foolishness of her all-too-human companions. That moral starch places her in opposition to Huck, who is never able to stand up to a system that robs individuals of their lives, and perhaps even more so to Tom, who is so interested in his own rise to power that he fully accepts the ideology of slavery and exploitation.

Why is Sam Clemens obsessed with Joan? Why does he insist on telling this story? Whose story is it anyway? For many readers, *Joan* is a failed book, a self-absorbed and misguided attempt by an author who, insecure and disappointed in his reputation as a humorist, felt driven to kindle some aesthetic sensibility within himself by turning to the serious topics of patriotism, martyrdom, and religious zeal. That interpretation was dominated by Van Wyck Brooks, one of the first to look for a way not only to categorize Mark Twain but also to split the writer Sam Clemens into pieces that when put back together didn't quite create a whole personality (we are all still struggling with that misguided approach). *Personal Recollections of Joan of Arc* was flawed; its narrator, Sieur Louis de Conte, was a symbol of the ruined storyteller. The attempt was a failure—both aesthetically *and* humorously. The book became the signpost of Sam Clemens' creative impotence. Such a splendid failure, however, cannot simply be ignored. *Joan of Arc* is not at its best as a representation of aesthetic value. It is stilted and uneven and reductive and derivative. It is, however, an open valve to the voice of alienation, a complex tale of a disappointing life told in a muffled, raspy, aged, disappointed voice.

Joan was reprinted as volume seventeen of the Oxford Mark Twain; ironically, Joan is seventeen when she dons her battle gear and marches out of Domremy with God's light in her eyes. But the question is whether critics have gotten any more sophisticated in their reading and interpretation of the story; after the interpretive arguments and shifting paradigms of the last two decades, are there any new thoughts? In his introduction of the Oxford Mark Twain volume, Justin Kaplan begins with this judgment:

> *Joan of Arc* . . . deserves respect, but for me, and I would guess for most contemporary readers, that respect comes with a certain degree of consternation. *Joan of Arc* is of less interest for its intrinsic literary quality than as a biographical crux, an event that illuminates the later life of a major American writer while not adding to his stature. It is the work of a deeply conflicted, intermittently fulfilled man and artist, a temporary resolution of the many disunities and identities of Samuel Clemens and Mark Twain.[1]

Kaplan here returns to the formula of the split personalities that have dominated much of Twain studies since the publication of his *Mr. Clemens and Mark Twain* (1966). There are echoes of Van Wyck Brooks' indictment in Kaplan's words—"a temporary resolution of the many disunities and identities of Samuel Clemens and Mark Twain." Kaplan oversimplifies the conflict in a resurgence of the Clemens/Twain dichotomy.

In the Oxford edition, to complete the cycle of comment on Twain's imminent failure, Kaplan's 1970 voice is bookended with Susan K. Harris' afterword. Harris offers a less stodgy reading that focuses on the relationship between Twain's ideological stance and the broad construction of his symbiotic intersection with premodern late-nineteenth and early twentieth-century culture. In Harris' words:

> Coming to attention during the latter part of the nineteenth century, the figure who could have been a symbol of the New Woman was as often co-opted by the conservative forces as by the liberal, becoming an anomaly used to highlight women's "essential" femininity and, most significantly, to support traditional sexual roles. . . . At heart a nineteenth-century "True" woman rather than a twentieth-century "New" one, Joan could be heralded as a leader whose heroism lay, paradoxically in her femininity, especially her feminine sacrifice of self for her country, her God, and her king.

Harris concludes, "Certainly this ideology informs Mark Twain's text."[2] Yes, it does. But does this enhance both our understanding and our appreciation of the story, especially in whether or how it illuminates what we know we think about Samuel Clemens or what we know we think about ourselves?

An element of stodginess erupts, a twist on the academic disease—a prizing of analytical distance over emotional strife. We can be so hypnotized by the trill and warble of cultural ideologies that we miss the record of and potential for individual pain. The specters of literary characters (of literary figures) oppose theory; theories are either easily forgotten or remain fixed—we can't read them any differently from one time to the next. Characters, however, live, die, are resurrected, become ghosts. We gain intimacy not with ideology but with characters through the link they offer to our own suffering. Culture is not family; ideology is neither gain nor loss of lover or friend. Or enemy. If every story is about the clash of ideologies, where does the human heart rest?

A good deal of criticism falls on deaf ears when we attempt to pour cultural analysis and theories of disaffection into general (lay?) readers. Readers are much more sophisticated and worldly and deeply wounded than we care to admit as we make facile and droll remarks about ideology and then feel that we have opened a new vista on literature. What opens that new vista is the emotional impact of reading and the ache of recognition readers nurse after reading. Readers are keenly tuned to stories of loss. They don't care about whether Mark Twain or Samuel Clemens is writing; the debate alienates them, and frankly it should alienate a lot of us. It's time we recognized the inherent complexity of the human mind and personality. The Twain/Clemens split has done little to enhance our understanding of the writer. It has stood in the way. It's time to get back to human stories; it is time that we cherish the ghosts that inhabit Clemens and his stories.

Harris does, I think, touch on the ghostly quality of Clemens' novel when, toward the end of her comments, she turns her attention to the value, character, and emotions of the storyteller:

> In *Personal Recollections of Joan of Arc* . . . Twain's male narrator is far more central to his [Twain's] concerns, especially his sense of alienation, than is the figure that gives the narrator reason for being. One of the last of his completed novels, *Joan of Arc* is marked by grief—not the grief de Conte consciously expresses about Joan's martyrdom, but the unconscious grief he represents. This is the grief of loss, of dislocation, of disaffection. It is the grief that accompanied the euphoria of late-nineteenth-century progress, and it is the grief that highlighted Mark Twain's own progress through life. It is the grief of the age, and like the other cultural discourses informing *Joan of Arc*, it reflects a communal experience refracted through one particular author's sensibility.[3]

Harris here gives us something good and tangible and lasting to hold—at least at the beginning of her statement. The value in *Joan of Arc* is in its presentation of an individual's "unconscious grief . . . the grief of loss, of dislocation, or disaffection." Therein, in fact, lies a tale—a ghost story, or rather, a story told by ghosts.

It is a story that focuses on the power of the night. It is not a power easily passed off as the incursion of the nightmare, the seduction of the incubus or succubus; rather, it is a fright that comes from an awareness of aloneness and a sense of the desolation that shock in those seconds between switching off the light and our eyes' adjustment to the darkness. There is terror in momentary blindness, a resonance of fear and uncertainty that lies in the heart of writers and their characters who confront the dark. There is no bump in this night. There is crash and burn. And the human soul is the victim of being compelled to face its own crushing solitude. Emily Dickinson had it right:

There is a solitude of space
A solitude of sea
A solitude of death, but these
Society shall be
Compared with that profounder site
That polar privacy
A soul admitted to itself—
Finite Infinity.

And so did Sam Clemens:

> It is quite true I took all the tragedies to myself; and tallied them off, in turn as they happened, saying to myself in each case, with a sigh, "Another one gone—and on my account; this ought to bring me to repentance; His patience will not always endure." And yet privately I thought that it would. That is, I believed in the daytime; but not the night. With the going down of the sun my faith failed, and the clammy fears gathered about my heart. It was then I repented. Those were awful nights, nights of despair, nights charged with bitterness and death. . . . In all my boyhood life I am not sure that I ever tried to lead a better life in the daytime—or wanted to. In my age I should never think of wishing to do such a thing. But in my age as in my youth, night brings me many a deep remorse. I realize from the cradle up I have been like the rest of the race—never quite sane in the night.[4]

Clemens knew the insanity of the night, and he injects his abiding sense of loss into a catalog of characters, especially when he allows those characters to tell their own stories, to give voice to their own isolation, aloneness, and disappointment. Huck Finn's voice comes immediately to mind. Louis de Conte also has just such a voice, a quiet, muffled, gravelly voice tuned by his reflection on loss. He offers a complex song of death in his *Personal Recollections of Joan of Arc.*

Like all death songs, de Conte's is a mix of disaffection, alienation, and disappointment. The insanity of the coming night prevents reconciliation. There is no spiritual reclamation; there is no joy. His story is not a celebration of Joan of Arc; it is a blast at humankind and (similarly, I think, to Hank Morgan's autobiography) a record of the gradual realization of possibilities lost:

> At bottom they were still under the spell of timorousness born of generations of unsuccess, and a lack of confidence in the way of treacheries of

> all sorts—for their kings had been treacherous to their great vassals and to their generals, and these in turn were treacherous to the head of the state and to each other. The soldiery found that they could depend utterly on Joan, and upon her alone. With her gone, everything was gone. She was the sun that melted the frozen torrents and set them boiling; with that sun removed, they froze again, and the army and all France became what they had been before, mere dead corpses—that and nothing more; incapable of thought, hope, ambition, or motion.[5]

This is very much like *A Connecticut Yankee*: a walk in the killing field that is daily life, a last look back, and like Lot's wife, the observer is stunned into the solidity of salt. De Conte's narrative is a walk in the company of ghosts that is ultimately a preparation for his own death. It is a tale of a reluctant soldier, one that is seasoned with momentary claims to humor and the distraction of short-lived, pyrrhic victories. Ultimately it is a story of individual disappointments—Joan's certainly (even her death is not what she wished it to be), but de Conte's especially.

Clearly, de Conte is displaced in time. As he moves away from the victories and the comradeship that united Joan, her friends, and her circle of advisors, his comments become more infused with sentiment and with a sense of lost youth: "How foolish we were; but we were young, you know, and youth hopeth all things, believeth all things" (II, 241); "Our imagination was on fire; we were delirious with pride and joy. For we were very young, as I have said" (II, 258). Aged eighty-two when he puts his memories to paper, de Conte can only look back at what he has lost with little sense of how history will judge his experiences or whether the work, the experience, and the love that so defined his life will have been in vain. He lives with his memories, but those memories are literally in ashes. "We are so strangely made," he writes, "the memories that could make us happy pass away; it is the memories that break our hearts that abide" (II, 259).

Like the crazed and obsessed narrator of Edgar Allan Poe's "Ligeia," Louis de Conte is left with the piercing memory of Joan's eyes. The story may be read as his growing restiveness under her gaze, his evolving sense of the purity in eyes destined to see God—and, it seems, destined to smite de Conte in his tracks:

> There was never but that one pair, there will never be another. Joan's eyes were deep and rich and wonderful beyond anything merely earthly. They spoke all the languages—they had no need of words. They produced all effects—and just by a glance: a glance that could convict a liar in his lie and make him confess it; that could bring down a proud man's pride and

> make him humble; that could put courage into a coward and strike dead the courage of the bravest; that could appease resentments and real hatreds; that could speak peace to storms and passion and be obeyed; that could make the doubter believe and the hopeless hope again; that could purify the impure mind; that could persuade—ah, there it is—persuasion! (I, 206)

And later:

> And her eyes—ah, you should have seen them and broken your hearts. . . . How capable they were, and how wonderful! Yes, at all times and in all circumstances they could express as by print every shade of the wide range of her moods. In them were hidden floods of gay sunshine, the softest and peacefulest twilights, and devastating storms and lightnings. Not in this world have there been others that were comparable to them. (II, 134)

Certainly, Joan gains strength from her voices, but what does she see with those eyes? And now, looking back some sixty years, what does de Conte see? Joan saw a direct and unchallengeable vision of unity through war. It's a frightening image of wounds and assaults, all undertaken for the greater glory. De Conte, looking back, sees a child's death. And he sees his own role in that death, and he is unable to reconcile the loss when so little was gained. His loss is personal. Not national. Not religious. He sees a childhood friend he loved engulfed—one way or the other—in the flames of political and religious zealotry. And he is tired. And he wants to die.

In a way, de Conte plays a dual role as both Kurt Vonnegut and Mary O'Hare. In the opening pages of *Slaughterhouse-Five,* Mary O'Hare takes after Vonnegut with a passion that lays him flat. She is angry about war and about the way men talk of war: "You'll pretend you were men instead of babies, and you'll be playing in the movies by Frank Sinatra and John Wayne or some of those other glamorous, war-loving, dirty old men. And war will just look wonderful, so we'll have a lot more of them. And they'll be fought by babies like the babies upstairs."[6] Her outburst becomes the subtitle for the book—"The Children's Crusade." What better description for de Conte's book, his history of the work of Joan of Arc, a child who takes it upon herself to answer the call to arms and who dies at the hands of men who are most concerned with their own place in the political and religious landscape—in short, with worldly "honor."

Relatively early in the story de Conte comments on the need for a less worldly and more spiritual honor and nobility: "For when a man's soul is starving, what does he care for meat and roof so he can get that nobler hunger fed?" (I, 91). Samuel Clemens, I suspect, would laugh. And maybe, by the end of his book, so does Louis de Conte. Vonnegut's first chapter of *Slaughterhouse-Five* ends with words that likely could have been penned by de Conte as he looked back at Joan: "People aren't supposed to look back. I'm certainly not going to do it anymore. I've finished my war book now. The next one I write is going to be fun. This one is a failure, and it had to be, since it was written by a pillar of salt."[7] De Conte's sense of his own failings season *Personal Recollections of Joan of Arc*, and that realization sets the tone for the sweeping sadness that is the book's center. This is his last chance to reconstruct his life, but instead of fashioning a story that casts him as a hero, de Conte offers himself as the deeply flawed chronicler of Joan's ascendancy. It is his one and only narrative of the life, of the lives. There will be no other. And he knows that he has failed to capture the reality of Joan because he has been incapable of admitting his love for her. However, Clemens added at least (depending on how you count) twelve additional books to his list after *Joan of Arc*. He kept writing, though he, like de Conte, struggled with the specter of his failure to satisfy his ambition for Joan's history.

Clemens, though, did succeed at resurrecting the light in Livy's eyes. Unlike critics who see Susy in the young Joan, it is a good deal more likely that Clemens was at this point using de Conte's hymn to the young saint as a comment on his growing fear of losing Livy, a fear that would take deep root and would blossom in regrets that shape his diaries of Adam and Eve and ultimately his autobiography.

All of that is prelude to the final blow, the tearing apart of the household with the departure of Isabel Lyon and Ralph Ashcroft, which would be followed too quickly by the death of Jean Clemens on Christmas Eve 1909. Sick to death (and sick of life), Clemens removed himself from Stormfield and took refuge in Bermuda during the early months of 1910 until his own physical decline hardened its grasp and he came home to Connecticut one last time to die.

Much has been made of Clemens' turn to political activism during his final years. Upon his return to the United States in 1900, Clemens embraced the anti-imperialist movement and devoted much of his writing to politics and polemics in the service of broad issues of human rights. His published writings turn markedly toward social issues, though the fiction that remained in manuscript at this death still clings to the domestic scene. Pieces such as "The Great Dark" and "Which Was the Dream?" focus his attention on the mutability of domestic circles and relations. Far from turning away from domesticity, Clemens threw himself into the domestic scene as he edited his autobiographical materials to give shape to the twenty-five installments that became "Chapters from My Autobiography" in the *North American Review* during 1906 and 1907. This final creative task drove Clemens as he attempted to right himself after Livy's death. It is clearly an important part of our understanding of Clemens' final years, and it is clearly an important statement of the value Clemens ascribed to domestic life and concerns. It is his attempt to reconnect with his dead wife and dead children, and it is his attempt (at least initially) to protect his daughters Clara and Jean from financial stress. The whole effort began as an experiment in biography. After being approached by Albert Bigelow Paine about the possibility of a formal biography, Clemens embraced the process of dictation as a way for Paine to gather information that would become part of his authorized story of the life.

Late in life, Samuel Clemens' view from the Hartford and Elmira porches, the view of Livy, Susy, Clara, Jean, and the small ghost of Langdon, along with ghosts of Henry Clemens and Jervis Langdon, excited in him both a joy of family and a fear of loss. He was sixty-nine when he began his autobiographical dictations. There he attempted a Hank Morgan effect by resurrecting Susy and conjuring memories of the Clemenses when the children were young.

Clemens deliberately recast the present by collaborating with his dead child. Using the text of the biography of him that Susy wrote when she was thirteen, Clemens created a conversation with his beloved Susy that rekindled, for the most part, the years before the girls found their way into adulthood and before both Susy and Livy died. Sam Clemens composed his autobiography motivated by the same sense of loss that prompted Hank Morgan to write his journal of Camelot and that prompted Suier de Conte to write his story of Joan of Arc. It was a way for him to return to the Hartford and Quarry Farm porches, a way to draw Livy and Langdon and Susy and Clara and Jean close once again.

One final and profound example: Jean Clemens, the youngest of the Clemens children, died unexpectedly at the final homestead, "Stormfield," in Redding, Connecticut. Clemens reached for a pen to work through his disappointment and his grief. In an essay titled "The Death of Jean" (published posthumously in 1911), Clemens writes:

> Why did I build this house two years ago? To shelter this vast emptiness? How foolish I was. But I shall stay in it. The spirits of the dead hallow a house, for me. It was not so with the other members of my family. Susy died in the house we built in Hartford. Mrs. Clemens would never enter it again. But it made the house dearer to me. I have entered it once since,

> when it was tenantless and silent and forlorn, but to me it was a holy place and beautiful. It seemed to me that the spirits of the dead were all about me, and would speak to me and welcome me if they could: Livy, and Susy, and George, and Henry Robinson, and Charles Dudley Warner. How good and kind they were, and how lovable their lives! In fancy I could see them all again. I could call the children back and hear them romp again with George [Griffin]—the peerless black ex-slave and children's idol who came one day—a flitting stranger—to wash windows, and stayed eighteen years. Until he died. Clara and Jean would never enter again the New York hotel which their mother had frequented in earlier days. They could not bear it. But I shall stay in this house. It is dearer to me to-night than ever it was before. Jean's spirit will make it beautiful for me always. Her lonely and tragic death—but I will not think of that now.[8]

A home, for Clemens, was the intersection between the past and the present. It gave entrance to emotions that could be achieved nowhere else. It was the spirit of compassion and love made manifest. Clemens remained in Redding; he did not make the trip to Elmira for Jean's burial. As he looked out into the snowstorm that blasted the day, this was his final paragraph:

> Five o'clock. It is all over.
>
> When Clara went away two weeks ago to live in Europe, it was hard, but I could bear it, for I had Jean left. I said *we* would be a family. We said we would be close comrades and happy—just we two. That fair dream was in my mind when Jean met me at the steamer last Monday; it was in my mind when she received me at the door last Tuesday evening. We were together; *we were a family*! the dream had come true—oh, preciously true, contentedly true, satisfyingly true! and remained true two whole days.
>
> And now? Now Jean is in her grave! In the grave—if I can believe it. God rest her sweet spirit.[9]

Combined, these two paragraphs return us to the loneliness of Huckleberry Finn and the despair of Hank Morgan and the weariness of Louis de Conte. There is no separation between creator and creation here. Clemens' emotion is real and vital and daunting in its clarity. It is heartfelt. It is passionate. And it is profoundly sad.

Sam Clemens' understanding of family and of place intersects for him on the porch as he recalls his children wrapped around him and as he looks straight at his own present and finds it inhabited by ghosts. His idea of himself as a writer and his concept of the value of story were shaped both by the intensity of family life and by his seeing the world not only as a place in which to live but also, and more importantly I think, as the place in which (his) children would live, and very late in life as the place where his grandchildren might live. At his death he did not know that a grandchild was only a few months from entering that world—a long story that is grist for another conversation.

Afterword

BEFORE HIS DEATH in 2011, Michael Kiskis began to write this book, which promised to reconfigure the field of Mark Twain studies by offering an alternative interpretation of Mark Twain's major fiction: not as realism, local color, or southwestern humor but as domestic novels, or more especially as satires or burlesques of domestic novels. Whereas authors of domestic melodrama idealized the courtly love tradition, valorized the family, and featured noble husbands and fathers and/or wives and mothers, Twain repeatedly undercut that tradition by portraying characters guilty of domestic violence, sentimental foolishness, and even infidelity. It was a remarkable move against the grain of Twain criticism, not least because it challenged us to look past the iconic "Saint Mark" who represented, as Michael put it, "an unchanging beacon of sense in a world of hurt and injustice": "If we treat Clemens as an icon, we set ourselves up for simplistic assumptions about the way we should use his writings to understand or affect our world. We then treat him as a savior for racial tolerance, ignoring that he was as profoundly conflicted as we are."[1]

Thus the raison d'être for this project, incomplete as it may be. It is rooted in the dark and neglected details of Samuel Clemens' life. The offspring of a loveless marriage, the child who became Mark Twain lived in a home over which the specter of violence continually hovered. His father, John Marshall Clemens, was not one to spare the rod and spoil the child, especially the slave child. "My father and I were always on the most distant terms when I was a boy—a sort of armed neutrality, so to speak," Sam remembered. "At irregular intervals this neutrality was broken, and suffering ensued; but I will be candid enough to say that the breaking and the suffering were always divided up with strict impartiality between us—which is to say, my father did the breaking, and I did the suffering."[2] He was whipped at least once for playing hooky from school.[3] In 1907, Clemens, in a magnanimous mood, recalled that his father "laid his hand upon me in punishment only twice in his life, and then not heavily; once for telling him a lie—which surprised me, and showed me how unsuspicious he was, for that was not my maiden effort. He punished me those two times only, and never any other member of the family at all; yet every now and then he cuffed our harmless slave boy, Lewis, for trifling little blunders and awkwardnesses."[4] In the manuscript of this reminiscence he had originally written "lashed" instead of "cuffed," but his wife while reading the manuscript noted, "I hate to have your father pictured as lashing a slave boy." Clemens responded to her prior to publication, "it's out, and my father is whitewashed."[5] But the change could not obscure the fact that John Marshall Clemens was a tyrannical master. On another occasion, after a slave named Jennie, long a member of the Clemens' household, grabbed a whip from the hand of Jane Lampton Clemens, Sam's mother, his father punished her by binding her wrists with a bridle rein and flogging her with a cowhide.[6] Clemens explained that his father "had passed his life among slaves from his cradle" and "acted from the custom of the time."[7] As Arthur Pettit adds, "apparently the 'custom of the time' was honored conscientiously in the Clemens household."[8] For the record, 16 percent of the three-thousand-plus slaves in Hannibal in 1860 were of mixed race—irrefutable evidence of the sexual exploitation of black women by their masters.[9] The peculiar institution was hardly the domestic ideal its apologists claimed. For the record, too, Hannibal during Sam Clemens' boyhood boasted its share of bawdy houses and prostitutes.

Predictably, from the earliest stages of his career, even as a teenager working in his brother Orion's Hannibal printshop, Sam wrote of violent and broken families. In "A Family Muss," his first substantial article in the *Hannibal Journal*, he detailed the behavior of an abusive husband and father.[10] In the ironically titled "Connubial Bliss," he observed that temperance advocates "do not look for" cautionary tales "among moderate drinkers" but to "the bloated, reeling drunkard" who "lays down the child, and 'lams' its mama."[11] In one of his most famous hoaxes, "A Bloody Massacre near Carson," written in October 1863 after joining the editorial staff of the Virginia City *Territorial Enterprise*, Clemens invented a blood-curdling tale about a deranged father who murders his wife and seven of his nine children. "I made the horrible details so carefully and conscientiously interesting," he allowed, "that the public simply devoured them greedily."[12] He wrote, for example, that the oldest daughter "must have taken refuge, in her terror, in the garret, as her body was found there, frightfully mutilated, and the knife with which her wounds had been inflicted still sticking in her side. The two girls, Julia and Emma, who had recovered sufficiently to be able to talk yesterday morning, state that their father knocked them down with a billet of wood and stamped on them."[13] In the first original article he published in the East under the Mark Twain pseudonym, "Those Blasted Children" in the New York *Sunday Mercury* for February 21, 1864, he ridiculed the Calvinist doctrine of innate depravity, facetiously suggesting if "young savages" stammer, they may be cured by removing the jaw. If they suffer from worms, "Administer a catfish three times a week. Keep the room very quiet; the fish won't bite if there is the least noise."[14] The bohemian actress Ada Clare, a habitué of Pfaff's beer cellar, accused him of "misunderstanding God's little people."[15] More likely he understood them very well indeed, especially the neglected and abused ones. Years later, he revamped the essay in a piece he contributed to *Childhood's Appeal*, a short-lived magazine conducted on behalf of the Massachusetts Society for the Prevention of Cruelty to Children. He facetiously suggested he was opposed to such an organization "when I have a baby downstairs that kept me awake several hours last night with no pretext for it but a desire to make trouble." He proposed that the editors of the magazine establish instead "a Society for the Prevention of Cruelty to Fathers."[16]

After leaving Nevada in late May 1864, Clemens became a local reporter for the San Francisco *Morning Call*, with a beat that included the criminal courts. Virginia City, with its city marshal and half-dozen police, hardly compared to the rough and tumble city by the bay, with its population of 115,000, sixty-two policemen, vice-ridden slums and red-light districts along the Barbary Coast, and history of vigilante justice. Clemens covered several cases of spousal abuse under such headlines as "A Wife-Smasher in Limbo" ("Cruelty to wives appears to be the besetting aim of a certain class of persons," one of whom broke "several of his wife's ribs" and bruised "her most unmercifully") and "Conjugal Infelicity" (about another of the class who pitched his wife "down a flight of stairs and followed up the fun by kicking her in the face and over the body").[17] He also reported on a case of extreme child abuse as the San Francisco correspondent of the *Territorial Enterprise* in December 1865,[18] and he described a visit to a New York institution for bootblacks, many of them boys orphaned by the Civil War, for the San Francisco *Alta California* shortly before leaving on the *Quaker City* tour of Europe and the Holy Land in the spring of 1867.[19]

Little wonder he depicted in his fiction so many flawed families and failed or failing marriages. We search in vain in Mark Twain's writings for portraits of happy, well-adjusted nuclear families. They don't exist in the world of his fiction, not even in the bucolic village of St. Petersburg. In *The Adventures of Tom Sawyer* Tom is an orphan in the care of an unmarried aunt and Huck has neither mother nor father. In the sequel, Huck announces in chapter 17 that the Grangerford clan "was a mighty nice family" who lived in "a mighty nice house, too"—but by the end of chapter 18 the elopement of Sophia Grangerford and Harney Shepherdson precipitates a mass slaughter of the males in the feuding families.[20] In *A Connecticut Yankee in King Arthur's Court,* the "lovely" Sir Lancelot might have made "a wife and children happy," but his affair with Guenever (her "furtive glances" at him "would have got him shot in Arkansas, to a dead certainty") and her broken marriage to King Arthur eventually spark a Holocaust if not Armageddon.[21] And if, as historians of the genre remind us, the novel is basically a story of heterosexual romance, where are the romances in Clemens' novels? They don't exist in *Huckleberry Finn* (surely not Uncle Silas and Aunt Sally!) or *The Prince and the Pauper.* The burlesque romance of Tom and Becky in *The Adventures of Tom Sawyer* depends for its humor upon an adult reader's recognition that the children mistake puppy love for mature devotion. (This is the best evidence, incidentally, that the novel is not primarily a book for juvenile readers.) Hank Morgan's wife, Sandy, in *A Connecticut Yankee* is little more than a caricature of a sentimental heroine, as ditzy as the character played on *Laugh-In* by the comedian Goldie Hawn. In *Pudd'nhead Wilson* the putative romances of the couples Rowena and Tom Driscoll and Roxy and Jasper are aborted before they are launched.

In fact, Twain often portrayed familial affection as a form of vulnerability, especially for slave parents. In debunking the racist notion that black people can't love their children as much as whites, a view best expressed by Marie St. Clare in *Uncle Tom's Cabin*, by his Hartford neighbor Harriet Beecher Stowe, he learned to appreciate the plight of the slave mother Cassy in the same novel. Cassy is weakened by motherhood, forced to capitulate to her master's demands lest he sell her (and his) children down the river. She is susceptible to coercion and extortion because she is a parent. Similarly, in *Huckleberry Finn* Jim must run away from Miss Watson and risk punishment because he fears she will sell him and he is desperate to keep his family intact. In "A True Story" (1874), mostly written in dialect and the first piece he published in the *Atlantic Monthly*; the Wilkes episode in *Huckleberry Finn*; and "The Pilgrims" chapter of *A Connecticut Yankee,* Clemens depicted the rending of slave families by auction and the anguish suffered by the parents. In *A Connecticut Yankee,* too, a peasant woman, another type of slave, is lynched because she stole to feed her child. And whereas Cassy kills her son to save him from the brutality of a slave life, Roxy in *Pudd'nhead Wilson* switches her son Chambers with the aristocratic white baby Tom Driscoll in order to prevent him from growing up a slave; that is, she must forfeit her role as his mother to protect him. She even allows him later to sell her back into slavery so that he can pay his gambling debts. In each case, the slave parent suffers a kind of punishment, sometimes even death, for loving a child.

But slave parents are not the only types of family members who are vulnerable in Clemens' fiction. Their misplaced affection for their putative uncles the Duke and the King exposes the Wilkes girls to their scam. Dobbs' disconsolate daughter arrives too late to prevent her father's murder by Sherburn. The imprisoned husband and wife in Morgan Le Fay's dungeon in *A Connecticut Yankee* are driven mad because, in consequence of their love, they are vulnerable to psychological torture. Judge Driscoll in *Pudd'nhead Wilson* is murdered by the usurper-Tom, his adoptive son, the same moral monster who sells his birthmother, Roxy, down the river. The list goes on. Significantly, too, several of Clemens' heroes—for example, Huck Finn, Pudd'nhead, and Joan of Arc—are free from the encumbrance of families and so are less exposed or vulnerable to danger than others. After faking his death, after all, Huck escapes from both the Widow and Pap; and at the close of the novel he flees Aunt Sally and her "sivilizing" ways. The three of them may hold different positions on the social scale, but they all represent the threat of domestication, and Huck wants nothing to do with any parental type.

References to physical abuse are ubiquitous in Clemens' books, especially abuse of women and children when inflicted by a husband or father or sadistic schoolmaster (in loco parentis). Even in his so-called hymn to boyhood, *The Adventures of Tom Sawyer*, there are a surprising number of allusions to corporal punishment, including Aunt Polly's threat to switch Tom for stealing jam and whacking him across the kitchen for ostensibly breaking a sugar bowl, Dobbins' swatting Tom for tardiness and stopping to talk to Huck Finn and "flaying" him for ostensibly tearing a page in his anatomy book, Mrs. Harper's confession she "knocked [Joe] sprawling" after he "busted a firecracker right under my nose," and Polly's admission she had "cracked [Tom's] head" with her thimble. Even after his "resurrection" in the midst of his own funeral, "Tom *got more cuffs* and kisses that day—according to Aunt Polly's varying moods—than he had earned before in a year" (my emphasis).[22] More to the point, Clemens portrayed the outcast Tom Canty as an abused child in *The Prince and the Pauper*: "All Offal Court was just such another hive as Canty's house. Drunkenness, riot and brawling were the order, there, every night and nearly all night long. Broken heads were as common as hunger in the place. . . . When he came home empty-handed at night, he knew his father would curse him and thrash him first, and that when he was done the awful grandmother would do it all over again and improve on it; and that away in the night his starving mother would slip to him stealthily with any miserable scrap or crust she had been able to save for him by going hungry herself, notwithstanding she was often caught in that sort of treason and soundly beaten for it by her husband."[23] However, Edward VI, the prince-in-disguise, in the course of the novel finds a worthy surrogate father in Miles Hendon.

But of course Clemens' best-known depiction of an abused child appears in *Adventures of Huckleberry Finn*. Pap is an abusive drunk who, Huck reports, "licked me" when he was liquored up and "used to always whale me when he was sober and could get his hands on me." He threatens to "cowhide me till I was black and blue" if Huck doesn't give him his share of the money he discovered in McDougal's Cave at the end of *Tom Sawyer*—another example of a Clemens character rendered vulnerable by a family tie. Huck escapes from Pap after he "got too handy with his hick'ry, and I couldn't stand it. I was all over welts." Even Jim, perhaps the most admirable father figure in the whole of Clemens' oeuvre, boxed his daughter's ears for what he thought was her willful refusal to "shet de do'" before discovering that she is deaf.[24]

Still, Clemens subscribed to the standard mid-Victorian ideologies of gender: the cult of true womanhood and the mythology of the "angel in the house," as his comment about Tom Canty's mother may suggest. He idealized his own mother, Jane Lampton Clemens, despite her inclination on at least one occasion to whip a slave. She had "a large heart; a heart so large that everybody's griefs and everybody's joys found welcome in it and hospitable accommodation," as he wrote shortly after her death in 1890. "She was of a sunshiny disposition, and her long life was mainly a holiday to her." She once prevented a "vicious devil" from lashing his daughter by giving him a tongue-lashing of her own, and he eventually "asked her pardon, and gave her his rope."[25] At the other extreme, he was appalled by the unladylike behavior of the libidinous actress Adah Isaacs Menken, who had four husbands, including the humorist George Henry Newell (aka Orpheus C. Kerr), and numerous lovers, including the elder Alexandre Dumas and Swinburne, before her death in 1868 at the age of thirty-three. She was no shrinking violet or delicate flower. "Somehow I begin to regard Menken's conduct as questionable, occasionally," he wrote a year before she died. "She has a passion for connecting herself with distinguished people, and then discarding them. . . . Heaven help us, what desperate chances she takes on her reputation!"[26]

Of Clemens' attitudes toward sexuality, especially during his years on the Comstock and in San Francisco, almost nothing is known. Maxwell Geismar has framed the problem best: "Despite all of Clemens' self-descriptions, and his obvious affinity for women, his pagan sense of pleasure and the flesh, and despite massive Twain scholarship, there is, as regards his sexual experiences or lack of them, a complete silence, and blank."[27] Dixon Wecter asserted that "a certain fear of sex . . . seems to lie at the root of Mark Twain's nature" and speculated that he was a virgin when he married in 1870 at the age of thirty-four.[28] That Clemens remained a virgin under these circumstances is fanciful at best. Louis J. Budd challenged the notion that Clemens was sexually repressed: Budd long ago described him as a "virile bachelor" and one of the "bully boys."[29] The available evidence tends to support Budd's view, even if it also betrays Clemens' mid-Victorian double standard. As he wrote his sister-in-law Mollie Clemens, the wife of his brother Orion, in late January 1862, "I don't mind sleeping with female servants as long as I am a bachelor—by *no* means—but *after* I marry, that sort of thing will be 'played out.'" He admonished Mollie not to "*hint* this depravity" to his mother and sister. He also assured her that he would not marry "until I can afford to have servants enough to leave my wife in the position for which I designed her, viz:—as a *companion*. Don't want to sleep with a three-fold Being who is cook, chambermaid and washerwoman all in one."[30] That is, he didn't mind sleeping with servants, but he didn't want his wife to be one.

He idealized the well-born Olivia Langdon Clemens, his wife for thirty-four years, no less. As he wrote a friend soon after their marriage, "She is the *best* girl, & the sweetest, & the gentlest, & the daintiest, & the most modest & unpretentious, & the wisest in all things she should be wise in & the most ignorant in all matters it would not grace her to know, & she is sensible & quick, & loving & faithful, forgiving, full of charity—& her beautiful life is ordered by a religion that is all kindliness & unselfishness. Before the gentle majesty of her purity all evil things & evil ways & evil deeds stand abashed,—then surrender."[31] During his visit to the Sandwich Islands in 1866, Clemens judged the native women against the domestic ideal of monogamy and modesty and found them failures on both counts. His opposition to women's suffrage as a young man was predicated on the standard domestic ideology of the era: that electioneering would corrupt pure women. As he only half-facetiously remonstrated in 1867, at the age of thirty-one: "Women, go your ways! Seek not to beguile us of our imperial privileges. Content yourself with your little feminine trifles—your babies, your benevolent societies and your knitting—and let your natural bosses do the voting. Stand back—you will be wanting to go to war next. We will let you teach school as much as you want to, and we will pay you half wages for it, too, but beware! we don't want you to crowd us too much."[32] Guy Cardwell has noted that the "arguments that Clemens marshaled against suffrage for women were both hoary and pseudochivalric. He found distasteful the very notion of women 'voting, and gabbling about politics, and electioneering.'"[33] Clemens even expressed approval of forced marriages on two occasions: aboard a ship in December 1866, when the captain discovered that a young couple was sailing together without benefit of clergy and he married them; and again in 1877, when Clemens insisted that one of his servants wed the man who was sneaking into her room at night. He may even have coerced his daughter Clara into marriage.[34] His sometimes inexplicable fascination with the "angelfish," a circle of prepubescent girls he drew around him late in life, ought to be seen through this lens: He continued to idealize feminine innocence until he died.

He was in his own right a doting if sometimes neglectful father. He was content to allow Olivia to be the disciplianarian to their three daughters. In his remarkable essay "What Ought He to Have Done?" (1885), Clemens makes clear that corporal punishment was administered in their home. "Whippings are not given in our house for revenge," he insisted, however. "They are not given for spite, nor ever in anger; they are given partly for punishment, but mainly by way of impressive reminder, and protector against a repetition of the offense. . . . The spanking is never a cruel one, but it is always an honest one. It hurts. If it hurts the child, imagine how it must hurt the mother."[35] The essay contains his fullest public comments on child-rearing and one of his earliest public comments about Livy—a measure of the privacy he wished to afford his family despite his own celebrity—and offers one of our few glimpses through the veil of "the sentimental image fostered by Clemens, Livy, and their daughters" of their domestic life.[36] In fact, Olivia often acted as the moral preceptor of her husband, whom she nicknamed "Youth" as if he were a child. She cautioned him, for example, in July 1877, as his friendship with Bret Harte was collapsing during the production of their play *Ah Sin*, "Don't say harsh things about Mr. Harte" and "don't talk against Mr. Harte."[37] Her warnings resonate with those of Miss Watson, the "tolerable slim old maid," who scolded Huck: "Don't put your feet up there, Huckleberry," and "Don't scrunch up like that, Huckleberry—set up straight."

Michael Kiskis understood all of this better and earlier than any of us. He did not suffer fools gladly, even if he sometimes played one. As he explained in an autobiographical essay published in 2005, in his own scholarship he gradually came to "emphasize [Clemens'] connection to the tradition of literary domesticity . . . especially . . . in how his marriage and his becoming a parent affect his writing and his observations of the world."[38] Like it or not, Michael became a reader-response critic. Fortunately, his wife, Ann Cady, has donated his collection of Twain books to the Center for Mark Twain Studies at Elmira College, and they are shelved at Quarry Farm, Clemens' summer retreat for most of his married life, now owned by the College. His glosses in the books reveal the focus of his reading interests, especially during the years immediately before his death. In his copy of *Mark Twain's Fables of Man* (1972) he flagged both "The Holy Children" and "Colloquy Between a Slum Child and a Moral Mentor." In his copy of Ron Powers' *Mark Twain: A Life*, he scored this excerpt from a letter Livy wrote Sam in late December 1871, with their premature infant son Langdon in delicate health: "Oh I do *love* the child so tenderly, if anything happens to me in the Spring you must never let him go away from you, keep him always with you, read and study and play with him, and I believe we should be re-united in the other world."[39] Langdon Clemens died seventeen months later in Livy's arms, and Sam unjustly blamed himself for the baby's death—because he took him on a carriage ride.[40] Next to the endnote for the quote in Powers' book, Michael wrote "Like Anne Bradstreet," a reference to Bradstreet's poem "Before the Birth of One of Her Children."

But more than any other of his works, *Adventures of Huckleberry Finn* was the template for Michael's reading of Clemens. As a reader-response critic would say, *Huckleberry Finn* is not the same novel in 1885 as it is in 1955 or 1985 or 2015. Or as Michael put it in another essay,

> Nineteenth-century readers saw *Huckleberry Finn* as a tale awash in the worries of the times and the child narrator as an unspoiled commentator on the vicissitudes of the social contract. Mid-twentieth-century readers saw the book as a clear endorsement of American exceptionalism and praised the novel for its clearly captured idea of American self-reliance. Late twentieth-century readers were drawn to the issue of race and the challenges of using the story of the white child and black runaway slave as common ground from which it might be possible to address a legacy of inequality and ornery prejudice. . . . Contemporary readers can hear Clemens' bass among his literary sisters as *Huck Finn* is linked to the nineteenth-century tradition of domesticity. Issues of family and the need to belong . . . have become more resonant. And the sufferings and the needs of the abused child take these days a greater share of our attention. Huck attracts new attention because we have become more attuned to the trauma of the street child, to the hopelessness sparked by the legacy of growing up without affection and stability and comfort.[41]

Or as he elsewhere succinctly predicted, "The next interpretive battle may be over Huck's influence on how we see and understand family relationships."[42] Certainly it is a more promising approach to the novel than the largely unproductive debate over whether or not *Huckleberry Finn* is a racist book. (For the record, the answer I always gave my students when they asked this question: yes and no.)

Michael's focus on domesticity in Twain's writings also mirrored his own concerns with issues of social class. He was born into an immigrant family and by his own testimony he struggled "to balance [his] hard won literary cultivation against a legacy of working class home life" and "to reconcile [his] entry into the educated/professional class" with his hardscrabble upbringing.[43] As so often is the case with academic research, his critical writing was informed by both his professional training and personal experience, and he ridiculed the "Neiman Marxists" or "Marxists in Reeboks." He closed this book by expressing a hope for "another conversation" with his readers, but unfortunately it was not to be. With his death, many of us lost a dear friend and all of us lost a wonderful teacher and dedicated scholar.

GARY SCHARNHORST
University of New Mexico

Notes

Foreword

Epigraph. *Mark Twain's Notebook*, ed. Albert Bigelow Paine (New York: Harper & Bros., 1935), 12.

1. *Mark Twain's Letters* (Berkeley: University of California Press, 1988), I:322–23.

2. Hamlin Hill, "Who Killed Mark Twain?" *American Literary Realism* 7 (Spring 1974), 119.

3. Mark Twain, *Adventures of Huckleberry Finn* (1885; repr., Berkeley: University of California Press, 1985), 1.

4. "Samuel Clemens and Me: Class, Mothers, and the Trauma of Loss," Quarry Farm Papers no. 8 (Elmira, NY: Elmira College Center for Mark Twain Studies, 2002).

5. Leo Marx, "Mr. Eliot, Mr. Trilling, and Huckleberry Finn," *American Scholar* 22 (Autumn 1953): 428.

6. Twain, *Adventures of Huckleberry Finn*, 4.

7. Twain, *Adventures of Huckleberry Finn*, xxvii.

8. Twain, *Adventures of Huckleberry Finn*, 23.

9. Twain, *Adventures of Huckleberry Finn*, 36.

10. Twain, *Adventures of Huckleberry Finn*, 362.

Introduction

Epigraph. *Mark Twain's Own Autobiography*, ed. Michael J. Kiskis (Madison: University of Wisconsin Press, 1990), 28.

1. Mark Twain, *The Adventures of Tom Sawyer* (Hartford, CT: American Publishing Co., 1876). Subsequent citations indicated parenthetically.

2. Steven Mintz, *Huck's Raft: A Story of American Childhood* (Cambridge, MA: Harvard University Press, 2006), 157.

Chapter 1

Epigraph. Mark Twain, *The Adventures of Tom Sawyer* (Hartford, CT: American Publishing Co.,1876), 19.

1. *Mark Twain's Letters* (Berkeley: University of California Press, 1987), I:359.

2. *Mark Twain's Letters* (Berkeley: University of California Press, 1994), IV:50.

3. *Mark Twain's Letters*, IV:51.

4. *Mark Twain's Letters*, IV:52.

5. *Mark Twain's Letters*, IV:157.

6. *Mark Twain's Letters*, IV:230.

7. *Mark Twain's Letters*, IV:239.

8. *Mark Twain's Letters*, IV:244.

9. *Mark Twain's Letters*, IV:442.

10. *Mark Twain's Letters*, IV:491.

11. *Mark Twain's Letters*, IV:499–500.

12. Jeffrey Steinbrink, *Getting to Be Mark Twain* (Berkeley: University of California Press, 1991), 190.

13. *Mark Twain's Letters* (Berkeley: University of California Press, 1987), V:44.

14. *Mark Twain's Letters*, V:98.

15. *Mark Twain's Own Autobiography*, 42–44.

16. *The Portable Mark Twain*, ed. Tom Quirk (New York: Penguin, 2004), 43–47.

17. *Mark Twain's Letters*, I:80–81.

18. Thomas Bailey Aldrich, *The Story of a Bad Boy* (Boston: Field, Osgood, 1869), 7–8.

19. *Mark Twain's Own Autobiography*, 51.

20. *Mark Twain-Howells Letters*, ed. Henry Nash Smith and William Gibson (Cambridge, MA: Belknap, 1960), 111.

21. *Mark Twain's Own Autobiography*, 191, 212.

22. *Mark Twain's Own Autobiography*, 191.

23. Mark Twain, *Huck Finn and Tom Sawyer among the Indians and Other Unfinished Stories* (Berkeley: University of California Press, 1989), 96.

24. Eric A. Shelman and Stephan Lazoritz, *The Mary Ellen Wilson Child Abuse Case and the Beginning of Children's Rights in 19th Century America* (Jefferson, NC: McFarland, 2005), 23.

25. Shelman and Lazoritz, *The Mary Ellen Wilson Child Abuse Case*, 168.

26. Jacob Riis, *Children of the Poor* (New York: C. Scribner, 1892), 143.

27. Shelman and Lazoritz, *The Mary Ellen Wilson Child Abuse Case*, 71.

28. Shelman and Lazoritz, *The Mary Ellen Wilson Child Abuse Case*, 70.

29. Shelman and Lazoritz, *The Mary Ellen Wilson Child Abuse Case*, 68.

30. Twain, *Adventures of Huckleberry Finn* (1885; repr., Berkeley: University of California Press, 1985), 30–31. Subsequent citations indicated parenthetically.

Chapter 2

Epigraph. Horace Bushnell, *Christian Nurture* (New York: C. Scribner, 1861), 94. Subsequent citations indicated parenthetically.

1. *Mark Twain's Letters*, IV:158.

2. *Mark Twain's Letters*, VI:504.

3. *Mark Twain-Howells Letters*, 144.

4. Leo Marx, *Huck Finn: A Case Study in Critical Controversy*, ed. Gerald Graff and James Phelan (New York: St. Martin's, 1995), 297.

5. Kurt Vonnegut, *Slaughterhouse-Five* (1969; repr., New York: Dell, 1991), 109.

Chapter 3

Epigraph. *Mark Twain's Notebooks and Journals, 1883–1891* (Berkeley: University of California Press, 1979), 191.

1. *Mark Twain's Letters*, I:10.

2. *The Prince and the Pauper* (New York: Harper & Bros., 1881), 3. Subsequent citations indicated parenthetically.

3. The newspaper reporter present when Mary Ellen Wilson was brought into court was Jacob Riis, *How the Other Half Lives* (1890; repr., New York: C. Scribner's Sons, 1914), 43.

4. Riis, *How the Other Half Lives*, 41.

Chapter 4

Epigraph. *A Connecticut Yankee in King Arthur's Court* (New York: Harper & Bros., 1889), 432. Subsequent citations indicated parenthetically.

1. Frances E. W. Harper, *Iola Leroy* (Philadelphia: Garrigues, 1892), 57.

2. Harper, *Iola Leroy*, 58.

3. Mark Twain, *The Tragedy of Pudd'nhead Wilson* (Hartford, CT: American Publishing Co., 1894), 32–33.

4. Twain, *Pudd'nhead Wilson*, 33.

Conclusion

Epigraph. *Mark Twain's Own Autobiography*, 249.

1. Kaplan, "Introduction," *Personal Recollections of Joan of Arc* (New York: Oxford University Press, 1996), xxxi.

2. Harris, "Afterword," *Personal Recollections of Joan of Arc* (New York: Oxford University Press, 1996), 5.

3. Harris, "Afterword," 10–11.

4. *Mark Twain's Own Autobiography*, 156.

5. *Personal Recollections of Joan of Arc* (New York: Harper & Bros., 1896), II:108. Subsequent citations indicated parenthetically.

6. Vonnegut, *Slaughterhouse-Five*, 14.

7. Vonnegut, *Slaughterhouse-Five*, 22.

8. *Mark Twain's Own Autobiography*, 249.

9. *Mark Twain's Own Autobiography*, 252.

Afterword

1. Michael Kiskis, "My Samuel Clemens," *Mark Twain Studies* 1 (October 2004): 10–12.

2. Mark Twain, "A Memory," *Galaxy* 10 (August 1870): 286.

3. Mark Twain, *The Innocents Abroad* (Hartford, CT: American Pub. Co., 1869), 177.

4. Mark Twain, *Following the Equator* (New York: Harper & Bros., 1897), 351–52.

5. Terrell Dempsey, *Searching for Jim: Slavery in Sam Clemens's World* (Columbia: University of Missouri Press, 2003), 87.

6. Albert Bigelow Paine, *Mark Twain: A Biography* (New York: Harper & Bros., 1912), iv.

7. Twain, *Following the Equator*, 352.

8. Pettit, "Mark Twain, Unreconstructed Southerner, and His View of the Negro, 1835–1860," *Rocky Mountain Social Science Journal* 7 (April 1970): 22.

9. Dempsey, *Searching for Jim*, 93.

10. Mark Twain, *Early Tales and Sketches*, ed. Edgar Marquess Branch and Robert H. Hirst (Berkeley: University of California Press, 1979), I:70–71.

11. Twain, *Early Tales and Sketches*, I:86–87.

12. Twain, "My Famous 'Bloody Massacre,'" *Galaxy* 9 (June 1870): 860.

13. Twain, *Early Tales and Sketches*, I:324–26.

14. Twain, *Early Tales and Sketches*, I:352–55.

15. Quoted in Franklin Walker, *San Francisco's Literary Frontier* (New York: Knopf, 1939), 174.

16. *Childhood's Appeal*, December 9, 1880; repr., "Babies as Burglar Alarms," *New York Times*, December 15, 1880, 2.

17. San Francisco *Morning Call*, July 14, 1864, 2; August 17, 1864, 3.

18. Reprinted in "Western," Salt Lake *Semi-Weekly Telegraph*, December 7, 1865, 1.

19. Twain, "The Bootblacks," San Francisco *Alta California*, July 14, 1867, 1.

20. Twain, *Adventures of Huckleberry Finn*, 136.

21. Twain, *A Connecticut Yankee in King Arthur's Court*, 386, 23.

22. Twain, *The Adventures of Tom Sawyer*, 18, 37, 69, 165, 131, 111, 147.

23. Twain, *The Prince and the Pauper*, 23–24.

24. Twain, *Huckleberry Finn*, 30, 201.

25. Twain, *Huck and Tom among the Indians*, 84.

26. Twain, "The Menken," San Francisco *Alta California*, June 16, 1867, 1.

27. Maxwell Geismar, *Mark Twain: An American Prophet* (New York: McGraw-Hill; 1970), 27.

28. Dixon Wecter, "Mark Twain," in *Literary History of the United States*, ed. Robert E. Spiller (New York: Macmillan, 1948), II:924; and "Introduction" to *The Love Letters of Mark Twain* (New York: Harper, 1949), 3–4.

29. Louis J. Budd, "Mark Twain Plays the Bachelor," *Western Humanities Review* 9 (Spring 1957): 157–67.

30. *Mark Twain's Letters*, I:145.

31. *Mark Twain's Letters*, IV:51–52.

32. "Female Suffrage," St. Louis *Missouri Democrat*, March 15, 1867, 4.

33. Cardwell, *The Man Who Was Mark Twain* (New Haven, CT: Yale University Press, 1991), 110.

34. Laura Skandera-Trombley, "Mark Twain's Annus Horribilis of 1908–1909," *American Literary Realm* 40 (Winter 2008): 114–36.

35. Twain, "What Ought He to Have Done?" *Christian Union*, July 16, 1885, 4.

36. Leland Krauth, "Biographers," in *Mark Twain Encyclopedia*, ed. J. R. LeMaster and James D. Wilson (New York: Garland, 1983), 84.

37. *The Love Letters of Mark Twain*, 203.

38. Michael Kiskis, "Jim Smiley's Yaller One-Eyed Cow; or, My Twenty-Four Years of Humor Studies," *Studies in American Humor* 13 (2005–6): 84.

39. Ron Powers, *Mark Twain: A Life* (New York: Free Press, 2005), 312; *Mark Twain's Letters*, IV:523.

40. Barbara Snedecor, "'He Was So Rarely Beautiful': Langdon Clemens," *American Literary Realism* 45 (Fall 2012): 60–69.

41. Kiskis, "My Samuel Clemens," 10–11.

42. Kiskis, "Twain and the Tradition of Literary Domesticity," in *Constructing Mark Twain: New Directions in Scholarship*, ed. Kiskis and Laura E. Skandera Trombley (Columbia: University of Missouri Press, 2001), 15.

43. Kiskis, "Jim Smiley's Yaller One-Eyed Cow," 85.

Index